Nottingham Transformed

Architecture and Regeneration for the New Millennium

Nottingham Transformed

Architecture and Regeneration for the New Millennium

Kenneth Powell
Photography by Martine Hamilton Knight

Foreword by Sir Paul Smith

First published 2006
by Merrell Publishers Limited

Head office:
81 Southwark Street
London SE1 0HX

New York office:
49 West 24th Street, 8th Floor
New York, NY 10010

www.merrellpublishers.com

PUBLISHER Hugh Merrell
EDITORIAL DIRECTOR Julian Honer
US DIRECTOR Joan Brookbank
SALES AND MARKETING MANAGER Kim Cope
SALES AND MARKETING EXECUTIVE Sarah Unitt
US SALES AND MARKETING ASSISTANT Elizabeth Choi
MANAGING EDITOR Anthea Snow
PROJECT EDITORS Claire Chandler and
Rosanna Fairhead
EDITOR Helen Miles
ART DIRECTOR Nicola Bailey
DESIGNER Paul Shinn
PRODUCTION MANAGER Michelle Draycott
PRODUCTION CONTROLLER Sadie Butler

British Library
Cataloguing-in-Publication Data:
Powell, Kenneth
Nottingham transformed : architecture and regeneration for the new millennium
1.Architecture – England – Nottingham
2.Urban renewal – England – Nottingham
3.Nottingham (England) – Buildings, structures, etc.
I.Title II.Hamilton Knight, Martine
720.9′4252
ISBN 1 85894 335 3

Produced by Merrell Publishers Limited
Designed by trockenbrot (Claudia Schenk and Anja Sicka)
Copy-edited by Mary Scott
Proof-read by Sarah Yates
Index by Hilary Bird

Printed and bound in Slovenia

Frontispiece: Evidence of the city's active building programme is provided by cranes, a temporary addition to Nottingham's elegant skyline.

Jacket front: Hopkins Architects' Inland Revenue Headquarters

Jacket back: Sky Mirror by Anish Kapoor in front of Marsh Grochowski's extension to the Nottingham Playhouse

Contents

Sponsors

bildurn

Bildurn (Properties) is a private Nottingham-based company engaged in high-quality urban centre regeneration projects such as Lace Market Square (p. 47) and Bottle Lane (pp. 52–53).

BWB Consulting is an integrated engineering, environmental and transportation consultancy. Established in Nottingham in 1990, the company now operates from five regional offices throughout the UK. BWB has contributed to a significant number of projects featured in this book.

Eastside and City Developments is a joint venture company made up of URUK and Explore Investments. It is delivering an ambitious £900 million urban regeneration project which will change the face of Nottingham's Eastside.

English Partnerships opened its East Midlands regional office in Nottingham in 2004. It is facilitating the city's urban renaissance through support for Nottingham Regeneration Ltd and specifically proposals for the creation of sustainable communities in the Waterside regeneration zone.

Experian is a global leader providing information solutions to organizations and consumers across many diverse industries. It has an unrivalled understanding of consumers, markets and economies spanning many geographical territories.

Franklin Ellis Architects, founded in 1993 and based in Nottingham, were the architects for Castle Wharf (pp. 68–69) and Willoughby House (pp. 162–65), the flagship store for Paul Smith.

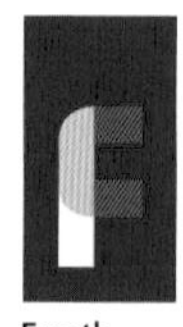

Freeth Cartwright LLP, a leading regional law firm with its headquarters in Nottingham, has been heavily involved in a wide range of prominent regeneration projects, including Castle Wharf (pp. 68–69), Bottle Lane (pp. 52–53) and the Trinity Square development.

Gleeds are international management and construction consultants with a strong regional base in Nottingham. They are delighted to be involved in the city's regeneration with major schemes from the Royal Centre to Bottle Lane (pp. 52–53) and the National Ice Arena (pp. 152–53). They are heavily involved in emerging projects such as the Eastside (pp. 98–99), the Midland Station regeneration (pp. 74–75) and many others in this book.

Lace Market Properties are proud to be involved in a number of projects appearing in this book. They create a new way of living in the city and are playing an essential part in the regeneration of Nottingham.

Monk Estates is a local developer responsible for Castle Wharf (pp. 68–69), Gamble Street regeneration, Trinity Square redevelopment, Royal Bank of Scotland headquarters, the Glass House and many new student accommodation schemes.

NDE

Nottingham Development Enterprise (NDE), a charity established in 1987, has an extensive track record of contributing to Nottingham's economic success, with projects including the remodelling of the Old Market Square (pp. 168–69), the Southside masterplan, the Midland Station regeneration (pp. 74–75) and the proposals for Victoria Embankment (pp. 152–53).

NRL is a public/private physical regeneration company, working across the conurbation and in the city's regeneration zones – Eastside, Waterside and Southside – to facilitate projects which deliver wider benefits for Nottingham.

The University of Nottingham

Dating from the late nineteenth century, the University has grown beyond its University Park Nottingham site to become a leading research institution with campuses in the UK, Malaysia and China. Its Nottingham Jubilee Campus is discussed on pp. 112–15 and 120–21.

Regeneration East Midlands

Regeneration East Midlands and Opun are collaborating to improve the quality of buildings and places throughout the region. Established in 2004, they are working with local, regional and national partners to improve regeneration practice through education, sharing and disseminating good practice, and encouraging investment in good design.

Westfield specializes in the management and development of shopping centres, and has over £18.9 billion of assets in 130 shopping centres across Australia, New Zealand, the USA and the UK, with more than 21,600 retailers and over 10 million sq m (108 million sq ft) of retail space. The redevelopment of Nottingham's Broad Marsh Centre is featured on pp. 166–67.

Nottingham City Council and Merrell are also appreciative of the generous contribution from **Tony and Christine Wilkinson.**

Foreword

by Sir Paul Smith

Nottingham is my home town, and I am very proud to have developed my business there.

This book means quite a lot to me: it covers a very important chapter in the development of the city, concentrating on how Nottingham has changed over the last twenty-five years and the imaginative plans for taking it forward.

There is a chapter on the Lace Market, once the vibrant heart of an international clothing and lace industry, and the place where I started out. Today the area has been transformed and its great buildings have been given a new lease of life, although sadly the lace and clothing for which Nottingham was famed are no longer made here.

The architectural story of Nottingham has not been a completely happy one. Magnificent landmarks such as Watson Fothergill's Black Boy Hotel were allowed to be demolished, and some of the new buildings in the city leave something to be desired.

The book shows, however, two things that are important to me: the conservation of and giving of new life to the many fantastic buildings that give Nottingham its distinctive character, and the promotion of outstanding quality in new architecture. I am very pleased that many of my favourite buildings, such as the former Boots department store, are featured, along with the impressive range of stunning new projects.

I am delighted to have played my part in the story of the transformation of the city, by restoring the wonderful Willoughby House on Low Pavement to its former glory and converting it into our new shop.

I hope that the book will inspire others to pursue imaginative new designs while respecting and conserving the best of the colourful past of a great place.

Paul Smith

Paul Smith

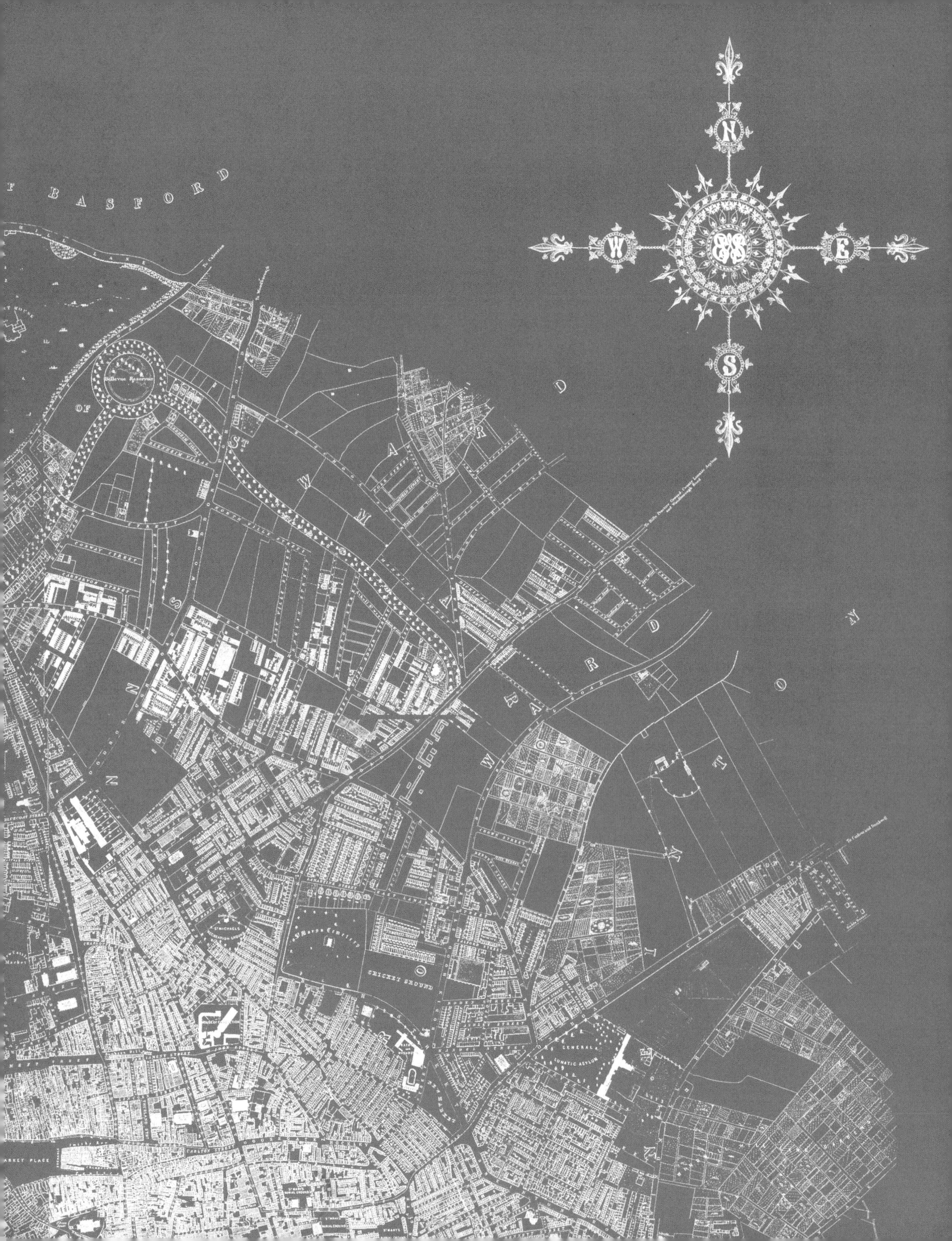

BASFORD
Bellevue Reservoir
General Cemetery
Cricket Ground
General Lunatic Asylum
Market Place
N
E
S
W

Introduction

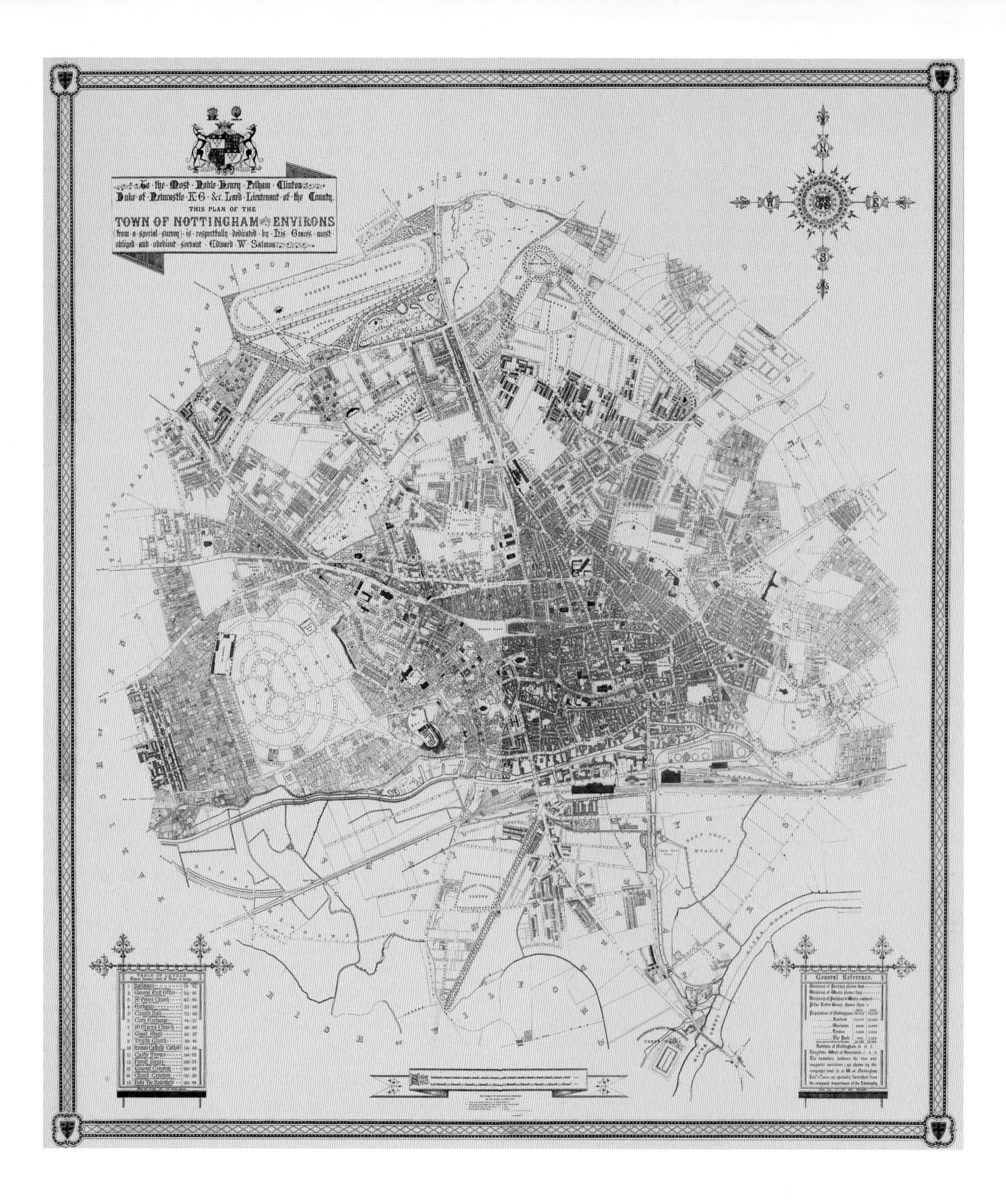

To the Most Noble Henry Pelham Clinton
Duke of Newcastle K.G. &c. Lord Lieutenant of the County.
THIS PLAN OF THE
TOWN OF NOTTINGHAM & ENVIRONS
(from a special survey) is respectfully dedicated by His Graces most obliged and obedient servant Edward W. Salmon.
PARISH OF BASFORD
LENTON
N
E
S
W
TABLE OF LEVELS
1 Railways 19 62
2 General Post Office 32 48
3 St Peters Church 45 69
4 Exchange 53 00
5 County Hall 72 49
6 Corn Exchange 74 27
7 St Marys Church 80 68
8 Grand Stand 86 57
9 Trinity Church 89 44
10 Roman Catholic Cathed! 114 68
11 Castle Terrace 144 75
12 Forest House 160 35
13 General Cemetery 180 05
14 Church Cemetery 181 26
15 Belle Vue Reservoir 261 04
General Reference.
Pillar Letter Boxes shewn thus
Population of Nottingham
Radford
Lenton
The Park

History of Nottingham

Mention Nottingham to many people and their thoughts will immediately turn to Robin Hood, Maid Marian and Friar Tuck, as well as their wily foe, the Sheriff of Nottingham. That there is still a Sheriff today reflects the fact that Nottingham has, like York and Norwich (and, among present-day 'core' cities, Bristol and Newcastle upon Tyne), a long history as a centre of governmental, commercial and cultural life.

Enclosed at least in part by a wall, with an important royal castle, monasteries and three parish churches, medieval Nottingham, close to the River Trent, was a hive of commercial activity. Cloth was a basic industry, as it was throughout late medieval England, but the production of alabaster statuary, exported all over Europe for religious use, was a distinctive local trade. The division of the historic core into the 'English' borough (the Saxon settlement on the hill around St Mary's church, roughly on the site of the present-day Lace Market) and the 'French' borough, laid out by the Normans and including what is now the Old Market Square, is detectable even today (see map). (The Old Market Square is a natural centre that has survived the urban reconstruction of the late twentieth century.)

The wall, the monasteries and most of the other medieval buildings have gone, but the castle, almost entirely rebuilt, still dominates the skyline, with the great tower of St Mary's hardly less prominent to the east. It is immediately clear that Nottingham is no parvenu among British cities. The natural drama of the site is, of course, a huge asset, with the castle on its sandstone escarpment overlooking the shallow bowl of the city centre and the Trent's flood plain beyond.

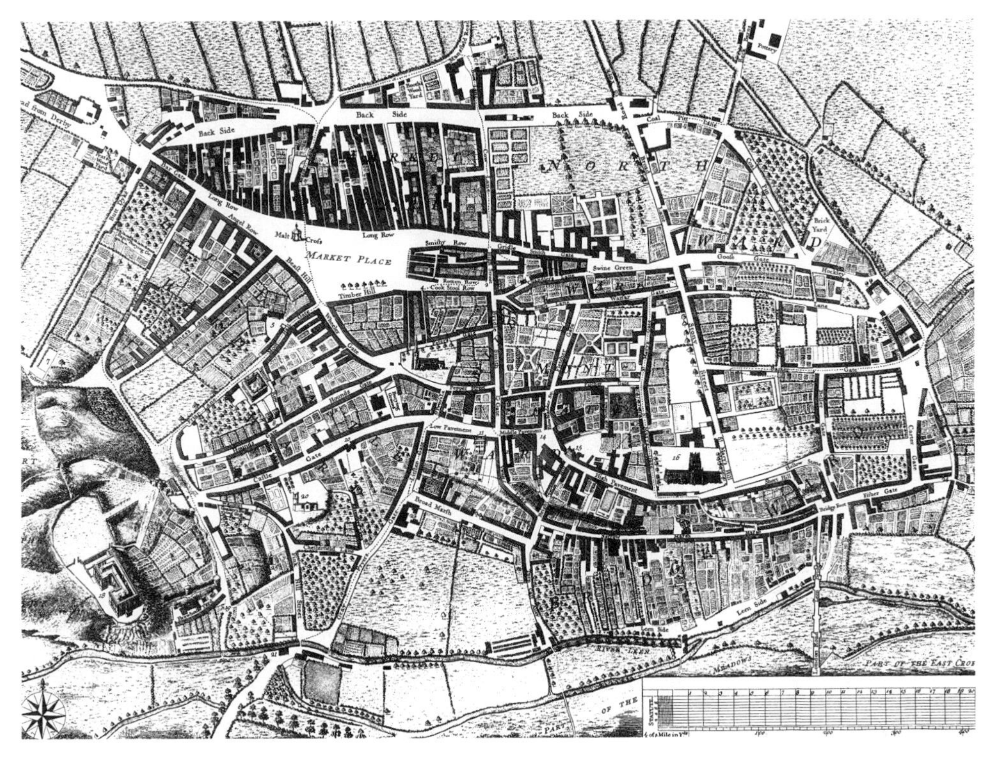

Edward Salmon's map of Nottingham, 1861 (opposite). Badder and Peat's "new plan of the town of Nottingham", 1744 (above). Fine Georgian housing can still be seen in the city, such as this building in St James's Street (above right), built in 1767 and once occupied by Cornelius Launder, High Sheriff of Nottinghamshire.

The outstanding Elizabethan house Wollaton Hall (above left), long used as a museum. The railway came to Nottingham in 1839, transforming the city's economy. The city is seen from the south-west, *c.* 1860 (above right). Watson Fothergill's 1893 Norris Ladies' Homes on Berridge Road (left).

A town of at most 5000 people in the Tudor period, Nottingham had more than doubled in size by the mid-eighteenth century. Georgian Nottingham was a modestly fashionable town, with assembly rooms and some impressive town houses built by the merchant class and local gentry. The population trebled again in the next half-century, and by 1851 Nottingham had 60,000 inhabitants. In the next decade, it grew by a staggering 30%. The principal engine of growth was initially the hosiery industry, supplying consumers across the country, and subsequently a commodity with which the city became indelibly associated in the Victorian period, lace. Fundamental to nineteenth-century female fashions, lace was to transform the look of the city. The first mechanized lace factories were outside the borough boundaries but by the end of the nineteenth century, the Lace Market had evolved as an area of imposing factories and warehouses, and has now become, in its turn, a flagship for the city's post-industrial regeneration. The railway, arriving in the city in 1839, allowed Nottingham's manufactures to be distributed increasingly nationwide. Readers of D.H. Lawrence (1885–1930), who was born in the nearby small town of Eastwood, will not need reminding that coal mining was important in the economy of the Nottingham region, and it was still even in recent decades. Lawrence was no enthusiast for the industrial city that formed the backcloth to his young life, commenting that "Nottingham is a vast place sprawling towards a million, and it is nothing more than an amorphous agglomeration."

Even the briefest account of the city's history cannot exclude a mention of the human misery that accompanied the process of industrialization. "The garden town became an urban slum," according to the centenary history of the city. By 1840, indeed, Nottingham's slums, generated by the influx of people in search of work in its growing industries, were reckoned amongst the worst in Britain, rivalling those of Salford and Leeds, and breeding frequent outbreaks of cholera. Well into the nineteenth century, the city remained within the stranglehold of its ancient boundaries, and only in the 1860s was the allocation of the surrounding open fields for development completed. The way in which this development took place was, as Nikolaus Pevsner remarked, "enlightened". A free-for-all building programme was not permitted. Alongside areas of dense working-class terraced housing, often of above-average quality for its time, spacious middle-class suburbs and areas of parkland were provided for: Nottingham's image as a green and

The castle remains the dominant feature of the city-centre skyline (above left). Between the wars Nottingham achieved the reputation of a progressive developer of public housing: seen here are Arnold Road, Bestwood (above) and Minver Crescent, Aspley (left).

leafy city, 'the garden town', was forged in the Victorian period. Some of the old slums were rapidly displaced by commercial development, though much that was old and quaint (and insanitary) survived well into the twentieth century. The construction of the boulevards in the 1880s underpinned the image of Nottingham as a progressive town in planning terms. Boundary extensions between the 1870s and the 1950s, though not as extensive as the then city fathers wished, took in much of the expanding suburbs, though a good deal of what is today perceived as 'Nottingham' remains formally outside the city, in the boroughs of Broxtowe, Rushcliffe, Gedling, Ashfield and Erewash (in Derbyshire), all contained within what may be defined as Greater Nottingham.

Nottingham's position as the capital of the East Midlands was assured when it gained city status in 1897, and by 1914 the population had risen to a quarter of a million. Every large British city has since been affected by the decline of traditional industries. In Nottingham, ready-made clothing seemed to be the answer to the decline of lace, but this industry too, a big employer even at the end of the twentieth century, has dwindled. (There were 5000 people, mostly women, making lace and clothing in the Lace Market in the 1970s, but this was less than one-fifth of the number working there in the 1890s.) By the 1930s, the city was dominated by 'Boots, baccy and bikes', with Boots the Chemist, Player's Tobacco and the Raleigh Cycle Company (later Raleigh Industries), all late Victorian in origin, as major employers. These were modern industries, conducted in locations beyond the city centre – Boots, for example, acquired its relatively salubrious Beeston site in 1926 and gradually transferred most of its activities there – and far removed from the polluting, declining heavy industries of the northern cities. "The town has some rough quarters still," wrote J.B. Priestley in 1934 of Nottingham, "but it is developing itself sensibly both in the old parts and the new."

The image of Nottingham as a go-ahead city persisted into the post-war years, though another image was reflected in Alan Sillitoe's classic novel *Saturday Night and Sunday Morning* (1958; later a film starring Albert Finney), a frank portrait of working-class life that shocked many at the time. ("Don't let the bastards grind you down" was the philosophy of the central character, womanizer and factory worker Arthur Seaton.) The back-cloth to the book is a city of factories, pubs and terraced houses. The housing programme launched energetically between the wars began to bite into the stock of outworn Victorian

Albert Finney in *Saturday Night and Sunday Morning* (1960, left). Slums such as these houses on Marple Street in St Ann's (above) persisted in Nottingham until the post-war years. The Great Central Railway's Victoria Station (1900, opposite) was demolished in the 1960s as part of the Beeching closure programme.

terraces in the Meadows and St Ann's, where clearance went on into the mid-1970s. These were genuinely deprived and depressing places, and the intentions of the planners and politicians were good, even if in hindsight the strategy of total clearance seems mistaken, destroying as it did communities along with buildings. Ken Coates and Richard Silburn's study of St Ann's, *Poverty: The Forgotten Englishmen* (1970), found the area, with its 10,000 houses and population of 30,000, "a slum which crawls on, wearily, over more than three hundred of Nottingham's dirtiest acres and more than eighty of its greediest years ... scarce trees stand as stunted hostages to rotting bricks and grey stones". More than 90% of houses had outside WCs, and almost as many lacked a bathroom. For Coates and Silburn, "romantic ideals of plebeian community" were out of joint with the reality of life in St Ann's. Clearly radical action was needed. There were efforts to save parts of the district, but the clean-sweep strategy prevailed, and terraces were replaced with low-rise houses which themselves soon became slums.

The period from the 1950s to the early 1970s was a time of rapid change in Nottingham. There were new roads, notably the highly contentious Maid Marian Way, slashing its way through the historic streets between the Lace Market and castle, while the local rail network was largely dismantled, with the total closure of the Great Central route and demolition of Victoria Station. The university grew, as did the polytechnic, now Nottingham Trent University, and education is now a major contributor to the city's economy. The Playhouse (1963) represented a major investment in culture, followed twenty years later by the refurbishment of the Theatre Royal and the construction of the attached concert hall, the two forming the Royal Centre, a bold piece of investment later emulated by Manchester and Birmingham.

The economic base of the city began to change in earnest during the 1980s. As late as the mid-1970s, Raleigh employed 7600 people, but by 2002 it had completely closed its Nottingham manufacturing base. Player's Tobacco vacated 92,900 sq m (1,000,000 sq ft) of space during the 1980s, moving all its operations to the New Horizon factory at Lenton and demolishing the vast Castle Tobacco factory in Radford, west of the city centre. The mining industry, still an important employer in the region after the war, went into terminal decline after the collapse of the 1984 miners' strike.

The prevailing philosophy of the Thatcher government elected in 1979 was one of non-intervention in the economy: 'uneconomic' industries were to be allowed to wither. Thatcherite orthodoxies were, however, balanced by the interventionist policies pursued by long-serving Environment Secretary Michael Heseltine, whose determination to tackle the social and environmental problems of the large cities fuelled the Urban Development Grant scheme and the later City Grants and Partnership Investment programme, both of which helped lever in investment for the regeneration of Nottingham's decaying Lace Market and the refurbishment of landmarks such as Newcastle House and the former Head Post Office.

New service industries, represented by companies such as Capital One and Experian, have now become significant employers, though the market for office space in Nottingham has always been relatively limited. The city centre

Radical road-building plans were central to the city's reconstruction strategy in the post-war period (this one, left, from 1965). System-built housing at Hyson Green (above), now demolished. A large concentration of high-rise housing formed part of the Victoria Centre redevelopment completed in 1972 (opposite).

looks prosperous, the shopping is excellent (Nottingham's centre ranks fifth among major shopping destinations in Britain and retailing is a major employer), and the bars and restaurants are booming. By 1997, 57,000 people worked in the city centre; retail floor space had increased by 40% in ten years and ten new hotels opened within five years. City-centre living is another major growth industry – around 40% of recent house building in Nottingham has taken place in the city centre – generating both the refurbishment of former industrial and commercial buildings and much new development.

The decision by Paul Smith – who, as a local entrepreneur, opened his first shop in Bridlesmith Gate in 1970, and is now an international fashion designer – to open his flagship store in the lovingly restored Willoughby House of *c.* 1738 on Low Pavement in 2004, was a landmark event for the city centre. Thirty years ago, it seemed that the new enclosed retail malls might threaten the survival of the established shopping streets, but these are more lively than ever, thanks to an infusion of new businesses: the pedestrianization of much of the city centre in the 1970s undoubtedly helped strengthen their appeal. The City 2000 initiative was launched in 1990, however, with a recognition that there was no excuse for complacency: the city centre needed to promote new retail and office opportunities, expand the centre beyond the 'concrete collar' of the inner ring-road, and improve accessibility and the quality of the overall environment. City 2000 launched city-centre management in Nottingham. The NET tram system (the first phase of which was inaugurated early in 2004) was a key element in city-centre regeneration, not just as a transport project but as a symbol of the city's aspirations, and was cast in a European model. The extension of pedestrianization on the key historic route between the castle and the Lace Market has boosted tourism, while the taming of Maid Marian Way, with subways removed and crossings created at ground level, has reconnected the castle to the Old Market Square.

The move away from road construction to investment in public transport began in earnest in the early 1970s, hastened by the rejection (after a public inquiry) of the proposed Robin Hood Way. Plans for such urban motorways, one of which was to run through the Park Estate, were

subsequently scrapped. The foundation in the late 1990s of the Greater Nottingham Transport Partnership marked a leap forward in coordinating public transport in the city, with proposals for two more tram lines, a new transport hub at Midland Station and the Turning Point scheme, all aimed at reducing car journeys across the centre and improving the pedestrian environment.

Nottingham's post-war problems – the decline of old industries, poor housing and vacant buildings – were real enough, though they did not compare with those of areas such as Merseyside, Tyneside or Salford. There were no vast tracts of concentrated dereliction. It was this fact, as much as the opposition of the local authority, that led the government to drop the idea of a development corporation for Nottingham along the lines of those set up in every other large city, including London's Docklands, where planning powers and large tranches of government money were handed over to the new corporations. In Nottingham, the City Council retained its planning powers intact, but the prospect of government intervention was a catalyst for the establishment of Nottingham Development Enterprise as a public/private partnership pioneering major development initiatives, including a tram system. The idea of public/private partnership soon became fundamental to major regeneration projects in the city – Boots, for example, was a key partner in the City Challenge project for St Ann's and Sneinton that attracted a £37.5 million government grant.

By the end of the twentieth century, the problem areas of the city, in terms of crime and antisocial behaviour, were often the housing schemes of the inter-war and post-war period, built on a tide of optimism, but which proved in some cases to be disastrous failures. Nottingham tried hard in the post-war period to retain its laurels as a progressive provider of rented housing – at one time, the local authority owned 62,000 houses and flats. (Today, council housing is vested in an 'arm's-length' company, Nottingham City Homes.) A hard-line approach was taken to the clearance of St Ann's and parts of the Meadows, though the outcome of clearance was not always what was hoped. The 800-plus flats at Basford, system-built and completed only in 1971, had been completely flattened as uninhabitable in less than fifteen years, along with similar developments at Balloon Woods and

The first phase of the tram system marked a major advance for the city's public transport (left). Maber Associates' Arena provides apartments in the heart of the Castle Conservation Area (above). The booking hall of the Midland Station, now the city's only mainline rail facility (opposite), which was restored in 1995 by Latham Architects and is now the subject of further plans.

Hyson Green. Cheverton Court in St Ann's was also demolished as part of an ongoing campaign of improvement in the area, involving the refurbishment of most of the housing.

In contrast to the depressing fate of some costly post-war housing experiments, the value (both commercial and social) of older buildings, whether fine listed structures or ordinary terraced houses, was increasingly realized from the 1970s onwards. Housing associations, coming to the fore as providers of 'social' housing following the decline of the local authority construction programme in the 1980s, have often driven the restoration of the city's run-down areas – the Guinness Trust's role in the regeneration of the Arboretum was crucial. With 60,000 students between them, Nottingham's two universities are hugely important to the city's economy as generators both of employment and of spending. Unfortunately, the impact of 'studentification' on some of the city's older suburbs has often been detrimental, with family housing converted, often poorly, for multi-occupation and the character of whole areas drastically changed. The problem is being addressed by recent legislation that will regulate (and, it is hoped, limit) the process, while the advent of purpose-built student housing projects such as the Student Exchange will relieve pressure on the older housing stock.

With the city centre set for continuing success as a place for locals to live, work and socialize, and as a growing tourist destination, the need for the regeneration of the inner suburbs becomes ever more apparent. The Meadows, for example, close to the city centre, remains a deprived area with the usual range of inner-city problems. On the other hand, it has considerable assets: the proximity of the River Trent, for example, where there are plans to develop the embankment as a major public amenity. The Meadows Gateway project is an initiative intended to reconnect the area to the city centre, with the Southside now a major growth area, significant redevelopment likely

around Midland Station, and the Eastside potentially emerging as a new district of the city. Redevelopment in the 1960s and 1970s disconnected areas such as the Meadows and St Ann's from the city: the aim now is to reconnect them.

The City Council's City Centre Masterplan looks forward to the development of the central area in the next decade, facing up squarely to the city's shortcomings as well as celebrating its many positive qualities. A better pedestrian environment is vital, it argues, with the spaces between buildings as important as the buildings themselves. In addition to the recast Old Market Square, eight new squares are planned, the first of which will be created in the Lace Market. Traffic is being tamed and public transport prioritized. The city's retail base will receive a major boost from the Broad Marsh and Trinity Square developments. Where new architecture is concerned, the aim is to encourage the very best. The importance of conservation to the perceived image of the city is acknowledged.

The recent tide of regeneration and investment in Nottingham has been as much, if not more, about conversion and reuse as about new building. The authors of *Nottingham Now*, published by the Nottingham Civic Society in 1975, compared the city to a patchwork quilt: "the material may be old, but still of good quality, some of it ordinary but pleasant: the historic buildings of every age and quality. Some of the material has to be new, but the pieces must fit into the overall design." Thirty years ago, these were quite radical sentiments, but the Nottingham of the twenty-first century is a dynamic city. As the City Centre Masterplan insists: "Nottingham must continue to be one of the most ambitious, innovative, creative and attractive of Britain's cities, to guarantee its continued success." It is as a city proud of its history, looking to the future but cherishing the best of the past, that Nottingham will play a lead role in the continuing renaissance of Britain's major cities.

St Mary's Church, Lace Market (above), one of the grandest medieval churches in the Midlands and a monument to Nottingham's medieval past. Wollaton Hall (opposite left) is the finest Elizabethan building in the Nottingham region. The Old Trip to Jerusalem (opposite right), a famous local hostelry at the base of Castle Rock, claimed to be the oldest inn in England.

Architecture in Nottingham

One building testifies eloquently to the prosperity of Nottingham in the Middle Ages. Of the three medieval churches, St Nicholas was destroyed in the Civil War and rebuilt in the late seventeenth century, and St Peter's, as Pevsner remarks, "might easily stand in any prosperous Notts village". St Mary's, however, is a town church on the scale of Norwich's St Peter Mancroft or Great St Mary's in Cambridge. Its complete reconstruction in the fifteenth century reflects the growing wealth of the town at that time. Holding its own on the skyline against the impact of nineteenth- and twentieth-century redevelopment, the church is one of a handful of Nottingham buildings of national, or even international, significance. George Gilbert Scott's sometime partner, W.B. Moffatt, carried out a thorough restoration from 1845 and completely rebuilt the west front. The work of a succession of able Victorian and early twentieth-century architects, notably Bodley & Garner and Temple Moore, has enriched the interior, with its wealth of monuments and stained glass, while Henry Wilson's south door is a major work by this great Arts and Crafts designer. There was a hope at the time that the church might become the cathedral of a new Anglican diocese, but the see for the East Midlands was, in the event, established at Southwell in 1884; Southwell Minster is now the cathedral of the renamed diocese of Southwell and Nottingham.

Pre-Georgian Nottingham is, the churches and castle apart, elusive in the modern city. Victorian and later slum clearance campaigns swept away hundreds of medieval and Tudor buildings: Thurland Hall, the most important medieval house in the town centre, for example, vanished in the 1830s. The Flying Horse Hotel and Salutation Inn are among the survivors. They are clearly timber-framed late medieval or early Tudor structures, though both have been grossly over-restored. (The Flying Horse was externally recast in the 1930s by D.G. Millett for Trust Houses, complete with pargeted plasterwork in an incongruously East Anglian manner.) The Bell Inn has medieval timbers behind its appealing early nineteenth-century frontage. The Old Trip to Jerusalem doubtless has medieval origins, though they are hard to discern among later additions. The Severns Building on Castle Gate survived in Middle Pavement until the 1960s, when it stood in the path of the Broad Marsh Centre. Conservation architect Freddie Charles re-erected it on Castle Gate; a worthy gesture, but the rescued fifteenth-century house looks embarrassingly self-conscious. Of the medieval castle, only fragments survive, notably the outer gateway. Wrecked in the Civil War, it was rebuilt as a grand Italianate mansion, comparable with those in the 'Dukeries' (an area of north

Watson Fothergill's Black Boy Hotel on Long Row (left) was one of the most tragic architectural losses of the 1970s. The Bromley House Library (opposite) is remaining evidence of the cultural vitality of Georgian Nottingham.

Nottinghamshire with a number of stately homes), by the 1st Duke of Newcastle, who is believed to have been architect as well as client for the project. In 1831 the castle was burnt out by rioters and abandoned, until the Victorian architect Thomas Chambers Hine (1813–1899) restored it as a museum in the 1870s. The city's greatest Tudor monument is far away from the city centre: Robert Smythson's Wollaton Hall is one of the most fantastic houses of the Elizabethan period, undervalued, perhaps, because of the loss of most of its interiors and its less than sympathetic museum use.

Georgian Nottingham, by contrast, remains tangible today. James Gandon's Shire Hall, completed in 1770, was a prestigious commission from an architect best known for the Dublin Custom House. The Georgian Assembly Rooms have vanished (apart from the 1830s façade) and the early eighteenth-century Exchange made way for Thomas Cecil Howitt's Council House in the 1920s. Abel Collin's Almshouses (1709) – "one of the best almshouses of its date in England", according to Pevsner – was, less forgivably, torn down in 1956, a victim of the disastrous Maid Marian Way. If surviving Georgian public buildings are few, the impressive run of town houses along Castle Gate, High Pavement and Low Pavement has a modest, county-town grandeur that evokes York rather than Leeds or Manchester. Bromley House, Angel Row, dating from 1752, was converted in 1820 for use as a subscription library (which continues today) and retains some notable interiors.

Ancient roots it may possess, but Nottingham is overwhelmingly a nineteenth- and twentieth-century city, created by industry. In the nineteenth century, Nottingham, like other large provincial towns, generated local architectural practices, responsible for most new building of any substance. Thomas Rickman, A.W.N. Pugin (architect of Nottingham's R.C. Cathedral of St Barnabas), Sir George Gilbert Scott, G.F. Bodley, J.L. Pearson, Alfred Waterhouse, and Lockwood and Mawson of Bradford all made forays into Nottingham, but most of the work went to locals. The work of T.C. Hine, whose family was active in the hosiery business, is omnipresent even today. Appointed surveyor to the Park Estate (where development had begun during the 1830s) in 1854, Hine made his mark on a planned suburban development of rare quality, which remains one of the most distinctive localities in Nottingham. Open-minded on issues of style, Hine moved easily from classicism to French Renaissance, neo-Tudor and neo-Gothic – his All Saints, Raleigh Street, is one of the most impressive of the city's nineteenth-century churches. The Adams Building is just one of a number of Lace Market warehouses designed by Hine, who was the natural choice for the extension of the Shire Hall and the reconstruction of the castle (burnt out in the 1831 riots) as a museum. Watson Fothergill (1841–1928) was of another generation, schooled in the strict Gothic Revival tradition but gradually developing a highly individual style which reflects the influence of Richard Norman Shaw and the 'Old English' fashion. Fothergill's many buildings in the city, picturesquely composed and intricately detailed, are easily recognizable, and the demolition in 1963 of his Black Boy Hotel on Long Row to make way for a drab new store was a local *cause célèbre*, hardening opposition to the process of comprehensive redevelopment.

Hine and Fothergill, dominating the local scene for decades, had no obvious successors, though the firm of Brewill & Bailey were more than competent Arts and Crafts designers – their church work included buildings for the Presbyterians on Mansfield Road and in West Bridgford. Architectural historicism lingered long in some circles: the church of St Margaret, Aspley Lane by E.H. Heazell was completed in 1936 but its neo-Perpendicular manner was fashionable forty years earlier. The churches of St Martin, Sherwood, and St Augustine (R.C.), Woodborough

GEORGIAN STAIRS

The Council House under construction showing the Goose Fair in progress in the old Market Square (top), and in a watercolour by Cyril Farey (above). It opened in 1929. The glazed dome (right) over the retail arcade forms part of the development.

Parts of T.C. Howitt's Council House development, incorporating an arcade (top) and formal entrance from the old Market Square (above). The former Boots store on High Street (right), a major work by Albert Nelson Bromley, recently restored by fashion chain Zara.

Road both reflect the fashion for the neo-Byzantine generated by J.F. Bentley's Westminster Cathedral (1895–1903). The next local architect to make an indelible mark on the city was T.C. Howitt (1889–1968). Howitt worked beyond Nottingham, designing major civic buildings in Newport (Gwent) and Birmingham, but he dominated the city's architectural scene from the 1920s until the late 1950s. The 1929 Council House is his most prominent work, a progressive building, Pevsner's biting criticisms notwithstanding, not for its style but for the way in which it integrated civic activities within the life of the city. The building's impressive retail arcade has the added advantage of bringing in rental income for the local authority. It was perhaps symptomatic that Nottingham was so slow in building such a civic monument: Hine's 1857 plan for an Exchange on the site was stillborn.

Howitt's career began in the office of Albert Nelson Bromley (1850–1934), a successful Nottingham practitioner whose working career, launched in partnership with Frederick Bakewell, extended into the 1920s. Bromley's major clients included the Nottingham School Board and the Boots Company – he was the architect of the splendid Boots store on High Street, later Maples, now occupied by the fashion chain Zara and one of the best Edwardian buildings in the city. Another, late work by Bromley stands opposite: formerly the National Provincial Bank, now the NatWest bank, on the corner of High Street and Smithy Row that is enveloped by Howitt's Council House, which occupies the rest of the block. Just before the First World War, Bromley visited the United States, where he became friendly with the major New York architect Cass Gilbert.

Perhaps Bromley's admiration of the United States rubbed off on his pupil – there is certainly something American about the Council House, which fuses transatlantic Neo-Grec with English Baroque. In 1920 Howitt joined the City Engineers' Department (effectively as city architect) specifically to work on the post-war

HOME
BREWERY
CO. LTD

Morley Horder's Trent Building (1928, opposite top) which forms the focus of the University of Nottingham's campus, and Howitt's Home Brewery at Daybrook (1938–39, opposite bottom), the only surviving part of the brewery complex. McMorran and Whitby's Cripps Hall (1957, right), one of the University of Nottingham's halls of residence.

housing programme. The Council House job was a direct commission; calls for a competition were ignored. In 1930 Howitt formally quit local authority employment to launch his own practice, with private commissions already in hand. The offices for Raleigh Cycles completed in 1931 were in the stripped, American-influenced classical manner that became the hallmark of Howitt's public and commercial architecture (with occasional inflections of Deco and the twentieth-century Dutch architect Dudok). (Howitt's housing, which has generally worn extremely well, though often despoiled by the replacement of windows and doors, remained in the Arts and Crafts/Garden City mould predominant in Britain until the Second World War.) Another prominent local client was the former Home Brewery, for which Howitt designed headquarters at Daybrook and dozens of new pubs. Howitt almost inevitably found work at the University of Nottingham after it acquired its charter in 1948. P. Morley Horder (nicknamed 'Holy Murder' by his assistants) had set the tone for the new Highfields campus with his Trent Building, opened in 1928. Howitt's Portland Building and Florence Nightingale Hall of the 1950s continued the traditionalist mood, which persisted into the 1960s when Basil Spence's first work on the campus overlapped with that of McMorran & Whitby (whose classicism, it must be said, had a progressive edge lacking in the work of Howitt). Towards the end of his career, in 1958, Howitt completed a city-centre landmark, NTU's Newton Building, which has always worried purist critics, who saw its style as perversely reactionary for the late 1950s; some have described it as Stalinist. But it has become a popular marker for the institution it serves.

Howitt's traditionalism did not go entirely unchallenged, though E. Vincent Harris's County Hall at West Bridgford, begun in 1937 but completed as late as the mid-1960s, was a highly competent exercise in civic classicism. Neo-Georgian was the preferred style for Nottingham's new schools during the 1930s, while the Police and Fire Service headquarters on Shakespeare Street, designed by city engineer R.M. Finch and opened in 1940, was another exercise in stripped municipal classicism. Modernist influences naturally pervaded the area of cinema and pub design. Eberlin & Derbyshire's roadhouse on Beechdale Road, completed in 1939, is a good example of the manner, while the Test Match pub in West Bridgford has been identified as a rare

1930s survivor, with largely intact interiors, and is now listed Grade II*. Albert Edgar Eberlin (1895–1977) was also responsible for the strikingly functionalist Daybrook Laundry on Mansfield Road, which A.P. Fawcett has described in an article as "the only building in Nottingham (if we ignore Owen Williams's Boots factory outside the city boundary) that emulates Le Corbusier's celebrated paradigm of modernity, La Maison Domino, of 1914". (Eberlin's work was generally eclectic and rarely outstanding, and it has been suggested that the laundry was actually the work of a talented assistant.) At Chilwell, Raymond Myerscough-Walker's house of 1937, built for the lace manufacturer R.J.T. Granger, was remarkable for its open plan and circular form, though it was largely constructed of traditional masonry rather than reinforced concrete. Now largely forgotten – because it has been either destroyed or mutilated – is the inter-war work of the Nottingham architect Reginald W. Cooper (1902–1969). Like so many architects of his era, Cooper was a stylistic opportunist, using a version of stripped classicism for the Oscroft service station (*c.* 1923; now a furniture showroom) on Castle Boulevard, a blocky Dudok manner for Butler's factory, and fully fledged Deco for the Metropole cinema in Sherwood, completed in 1937. The showroom and service station in Derby, also designed for Messrs Oscroft, was a classic piece of Deco that would not have looked out of place on Sunset Boulevard.

F.A. Broadhead's Newcastle House (built as Viyella House in 1932–33) was more American than European in inspiration, its large-span concrete floors between mushroom columns constructed by a US-owned specialist company. Viyella was itself in American ownership at the time. When Boots acquired its 121 ha (300 acre) site at Beeston in 1926, it was part of the American-owned United Drugs Company (the American connection was subsequently severed). The two major buildings at Beeston designed by Sir Owen Williams and now listed Grade I are among the finest twentieth-century industrial structures in Britain, drawing inspiration from the work of the American firm Albert Kahn Associates. The 'Wets' factory (D10), a "crystal palace of industry" completed in 1932, is as visually stunning as it is structurally impressive, and has become an icon of modern design. The form of the building was a rigorous response to the functional demands of the production process, with great lightwells housing production and packing facilities at ground-floor level, and upper floors used for storage and serviced by a series of chutes and conveyor belts. The central packing hall, 182 m (600 ft) long,

Gerald Goalen's Church of the Good Shepherd, Woodthorpe (opposite), one of the outstanding 1960s buildings in the Nottingham area. Two Modern Movement landmarks of the 1930s were Raymond Myerscough-Walker's house at Chilwell (above) and A.E. Eberlin's Daybrook Laundry on Mansfield Road (left).

crossed by a series of bridges and top-lit, is one of the great modern interiors of Europe. Externally, the building was entirely clad in patent glazing between the cantilevered concrete floor slabs, producing a strikingly sleek aesthetic, though aesthetics were not Williams's concern. (The exterior was reclad as part of a recent refurbishment overseen by English Heritage; see pp. 82–85.) Boots' 'Drys' building (D6), also designed by Williams and built in 1935–38, may lack the instant visual impact of D10, but as a structure it is even more remarkable. The way in which the floors are cantilevered out (by up to 14.5 m/48 ft) over ground-level loading bays, along with the suspension of the main beams from huge hangars at roof level, reflects Williams's quest for perennial structural innovation, moving beyond the well-tried flat-slab construction of D10.

Boots was to continue as an enlightened patron of architecture in the post-war period. The new head offices (D90) at Beeston, designed by the American practice of Skidmore, Owings & Merrill in association with leading British practice YRM and completed in 1968, was a highly progressive move, producing largely open-plan office space, rare in 1960s Britain. Listed Grade II* in 1996, the building has been sensitively extended and refurbished by design consultancy DEGW (see pp. 86–89). The other outstanding 1960s building in Nottingham (leaving aside Gerald Goalen's Catholic Church of the Good Shepherd at Woodthorpe, outside the city boundary) is, of course, the Playhouse, completed in 1963 and the masterpiece of Peter Moro (who had worked on London's Royal Festival Hall with Leslie Martin). The theatre was built with the windfall that came to the local authority from the sale of the local gas industry. Its success as a performance venue derives from its ability to adapt to either conventional (proscenium arch) or thrust-stage productions. Equally successful is the way in which the exterior of the building responds to its context and breaks down the divide between outside and inside. Julian Marsh's extension (see pp. 132–35) has further developed the relationship of the theatre with the city, creating an external space dominated by Anish Kapoor's Sky Mirror (2001).

These outstanding projects apart, the 1960s was a decade when the quantity of new building was not matched by its quality. "Unprepossessing" was Pevsner's comment on the Broad Marsh Centre, construction of which began in 1965. The Centre was architecturally no worse than many similar developments in British cities, but its brutal impact on the city, replacing characterful

Drury Hill (opposite), a characteristic old city thoroughfare, was controversially demolished to make way for the Broad Marsh Centre. Watson Fothergill's former *Nottingham Express* offices (right and below left) and Adamson and Kinns' Elite Cinema (below right) were cleaned and restored as part of the Operation Clean-Up programme launched in 1980.

streets, notably the much-loved Drury Hill, with dismal enclosed malls, was unforgivable. Its planned demolition will be regretted by nobody. Along with the new office blocks lining Maid Marian Way and jostling their way into the Old Market Square, it is seen as a negative presence in the city. The 1972 Victoria Centre, replacing the station of the same name by Midland Station architect A.E. Lambert (who also designed the Albert Hall of 1907–09 in North Circus Street as a central hall for the Methodists), is chiefly notable for the incorporation of a substantial amount of residential space arranged in tall blocks that have a coarse drama of their own. The pace of change in the 1950s and 1960s, and the destruction of so much that was familiar, generated a growing public interest in planning and architectural issues. The Nottingham Civic Society was founded in 1961 and has been an important voice for four decades, both as a campaigning body and for its research and publishing activities. Ken Brand's studies of Hine and Fothergill, for example, were the first publications on nineteenth-century Nottingham architects. Public appreciation of the city's historic architecture was stimulated by the concerted campaign launched by the city in 1980 (and extending over a decade at a cost of more than £10 million) under the 'Operation Clean-Up' banner. Grimy façades were cleaned to reveal decorative ensembles of carved stone and colourful brick, and long-derelict sites were reclaimed – in total, more than 3500 buildings and sites were tackled, with generous subventions coming from central government.

During the 1960s, a period of rapid expansion for higher education, the University of Nottingham (given the Royal Charter that finally allowed it to award its own degrees as late as 1948) turned decisively to Modernism with a series of buildings designed by Basil Spence and the practice of Renton Howard Wood (later Renton Howard Wood Levin), which took up Spence's mantle after his death. For the first time, the university went high-rise, with the 1964 Tower Building. With the completion of the Hallward Library in 1973 by architects Faulkner-Brown, Hendy, Watkinson and Stonor, the university acquired a modern building of unequivocally outstanding quality. As Faulkner Browns, the practice returned to the campus in the 1990s to design the delightful swimming pool. By the 1990s, Post-modernism had made its mark on the campus, notably with Graham Brown's Djanogly Arts Centre, but the great landmark development of the millennium was the new Jubilee Campus by Hopkins Architects, then Michael Hopkins & Partners. Its high architectural and landscape quality apart, the Jubilee project marked the re-engagement of the university with the city, using a classic 'brownfield' site. (The former University College in Shakespeare Street, where D.H. Lawrence studied, was handed to the city in 1928 and later became the core of Trent Polytechnic, now Nottingham Trent University.)

The Jubilee Campus, along with Hopkins Architects' earlier Inland Revenue headquarters (won in a 1992 competition), put Nottingham back on the architectural map of Britain. The 1970s had been a period of economic recession and political uncertainty, though the decade began with the completion of a major new industrial monument, the Horizon factory at Lenton, designed by Arup Associates for John Player & Sons and providing a vast, column-free internal production space. (The huge Player's factory complex at nearby Radford, including the architecturally impressive 1932 block on Radford Boulevard, was regrettably demolished in the 1980s.) The Castle Park factory/warehouse development, initially a Farrell/Grimshaw project but completed by Nicholas Grimshaw after his split with Terry Farrell in 1980, was hailed by Peter Davey of *Architectural Review* as a sign that Nottingham was turning its back on "dismal nineteenth-century industrial clutter". The silver shed, 260 m (850 ft) long, with its distinctive green service towers, heralded "a cleaner, saner age. ... The Modern Movement is alive, well and doing what it's best at in Nottingham."

Growing public antipathy to comprehensive redevelopment, reinforced by the rise of conservation, community and environmental lobbies, had a growing impact on planning policies from 1970 onwards, with many more buildings protected by listing or the designation of Conservation Areas – Nottingham City Council had designated nine by 1975. The result was a greatly increased emphasis on the conversion and reuse of old buildings, which has underpinned the regeneration of the Lace Market and become a prime ingredient in the development scene of the early twenty-first century. The mechanics for the renaissance of the Lace Market were significant for the city's future regeneration, with the public/private Lace Market Development Company forming the template for Nottingham Regeneration Limited, established in 1998 to progress physical regeneration of a range of sites, with a particular focus on the Waterside and the provision of new employment space.

The "dismal industrial clutter" gradually became a valued commodity, though in some cases – the former Great Northern Station and warehouses and Lambert's factory, for example – there were hard conservation battles to fight. The most prominent public project of the 1970s was RHWL's restoration and extension of the Victorian Theatre Royal, completed in 1978, interesting for the bold statement made by the new additions. In new architecture, there was a growing concern for context and, with Post-modernism, for historical reference – sometimes with dubious consequences. One of the pioneering projects in this mould, and one that has worn well, is Cullen Carter & Hill Architects' Halifax Place housing in St Mary's Gate, just west of St Mary's Church. The development of sixty apartments and four houses, completed in 1982, was built by the Bridge Housing Society, a housing association with its origins in the Civic Society and a distinguished group of trustees including the urban historian Maurice Barley. The scheme is neatly detailed in brick, with pitched roofs, intelligently drawing on the local vernacular.

The best architecture of the last twenty-five years forms the subject matter of this book. Today, as in Victorian times, local practices retain a strong hold on the city, though none enjoys the dominant position of a Hine or a Howitt. In recent years, practices from beyond the region have made their mark on Nottingham, a process prefigured by the patronage of Boots and Player's but beginning in earnest with Hopkins Architects' projects for the Inland Revenue and the University of Nottingham. The city's architectural parameters look set to expand further as it looks forward to exciting developments by Caruso St John, Benson + Forsyth, Make Architects and others.

Renton Howard Wood's 1964 Tower Building (above left) at the University of Nottingham. The Castle Park warehouse and factory development (above right), started by Farrell/Grimshaw, completed by Grimshaw. Cullen Carter & Hill's Halifax Place housing (opposite), completed in 1982.

Nottingham Now

CITY CENTRE

1 Castle Wharf
2 Newcastle House
3 Inland Revenue
4 Park Rock, Castle Boulevard
5 Royal Standard Place and Arena Apartments
6 Hart's Hotel
7 Capital One: Loxley House and Trent House
8 Holmes Place, Great Northern (Low-level) Station
9 Eastside
10 Broad Marsh Shopping Centre
11 Adams Building
12 Galleries of Justice, Shire Hall
13 Pitcher and Piano
14 Centre for Contemporary Art Nottingham (CCAN)
15 Bottle Lane
16 Lace Market Square
17 Old Market Square and Council House
18 Castle Park
19 Zara
20 Newton and Arkwright Buildings, Nottingham Trent University
21 Lace Market Hotel
22 One Fletcher Gate
23 Commerce Square
24 St Mary's Church
25 Magistrates' Courts
26 John A. Stephens, Castle Meadow Road
27 Nottingham Station
28 Nottingham Castle
29 Royal Centre: Concert Hall and Theatre Royal
30 Broadway
31 Cornerhouse
32 National Ice Arena
33 Paul Smith, Willoughby House

GREATER NOTTINGHAM

1 City Hospital Breast Institute
2 Djanogly City Academy
3 New Art Exchange
4 Jubilee Campus, University of Nottingham
5 Jubilee Campus, Phase 2, University of Nottingham
6 Main Campus, University of Nottingham
7 Visitor Centre, Attenborough Nature Reserve
8 Trent Bridge Cricket Ground
9 Nottingham Waterside
10 Experian Fairham House
11 Experian Landmark House

The Lace Market

The Lace Market

In the 1970s, the Lace Market was an area rich in history but with no obvious future, or so it seemed to many. Once the dynamic heart of the lace industry, Nottingham's staple trade, its decline had begun after the First World War and continued in the depression years. The most magnificent of the great warehouses there, the Adams Building, closed in 1950; it was later sold off for a pittance and became a poorly maintained warren of small businesses. In fact, as late as the 1970s, around 5000 textile and clothing workers were employed in the area and there were hopes for a time of reviving it as a centre of the fashion trade. But it was not to be. By the mid-1990s, the textile industry was virtually defunct.

During the 1960s, the obvious solution to some was total clearance. Some buildings were demolished and the blight cast by new road plans deterred investment in others. Derelict sites abounded and were used for car parking. The designation of the Lace Market as a Conservation Area in 1969 and the listing, a few years later, of some thirty-five buildings there

Stoney Street *c.* 1910 (above) is evidence of a still bustling Lace Market, even then in significant decline. Warehouses on Broadway in the 1930s (right), when the area was still part of the city's industrial hub. The Lace Market, its warehouses converted, has re-emerged in recent years (opposite).

the g@llery

Church Lukas's One Fletcher Gate development (above left) forms a new gateway to the Lace Market. View along High Pavement (above) showing the Lace Market Hotel on the right. The former Shire Hall, now housing the Galleries of Justice (left). Commerce Square has been revitalized as part of the regeneration of the area (far left).

signalled a change of heart, but it was not clear how the long-overdue process of regeneration and restoration could be funded. The 1975 conservation plan published by the city envisaged a mix of rehabilitation and selective demolition. The establishment in 1976 of a Town Scheme, one of the first for an industrial area and funded by the Historic Buildings Council, provided an impetus to repair and reuse. Drawing on a variety of funding sources, the regeneration campaign got underway and, by the late 1980s, much had been achieved in terms of the cleaning, repair and reuse of many buildings and the improvement of the overall environment of the area. The establishment of the public/private partnership Lace Market Development Company in 1990 was another landmark.

The first major housing project here was the Halifax Place development, completed in 1982 by the Bridge Housing Society. It was more than a decade later, however, that the boom in city-centre living launched a developer scramble for buildings and sites in the area. The flagship of the Lace Market, the Adams Building by T.C. Hine, found an appropriately public use after being briefly considered as the new head-quarters of English Heritage. The renaissance of Commerce Square, a characterful but long-derelict complex of factory and warehouse buildings that sits on the cliff at the southern edge of the Lace Market, was another regeneration landmark. Architects HLM, working with structural engineer Ward Cole, faced substantial problems in adapting the buildings,

Commerce Square, set on the edge of the dramatic sandstone escarpment where the city was first settled, has preserved and enhanced this celebrated piece of the town's landscape. St Mary's is seen in the background.

some of them eight storeys high, to residential use and creating underground parking beneath them. The glazed atrium at the centre of the development channels natural light into the heart of the site. The predominance of brick as an original building material in the Lace Market (a small number of public buildings apart) has been reflected in new development there. Church Lukas's The Point, completed in 2001 and containing thirty-nine apartments, takes its cue from Nottingham's warehouse vernacular but interprets it in contemporary language. The scale is appropriate and the detailing suitably straightforward, and the building reads well in distant views of the Lace Market. The same practice's One Fletcher Gate, completed in 2004, forms a gateway to the area, with 101 flats, and shops, bars and restaurants at street level. The language of this project is more obviously monumental, but then it addresses the city centre as well as the Lace Market. The development frames a fine new view of the Adams Building and connects to the Lace Market Square development, which provides a much-needed public space in the Lace Market quarter and an appropriate setting for Hine's fine building. The Lace Market Square scheme provides for two new buildings, designed by Franklin Ellis Architects, enclosing the northern and western edges of the space, with apartments on upper floors and shops, restaurants and other uses at street level, giving the scheme an 'active' frontage.

While St Mary's Church continues in use as the mother church of Nottingham, the Unitarian

The former High Pavement chapel, now converted to the Pitcher & Piano bar (left) by The Design Solution. The main courtroom in the former Shire Hall has been preserved (top); it was remodelled by T.C. Hine in the late nineteenth century after a major fire. The bar area of the Lace Market Hotel (above).

High Pavement Chapel (Stuart Colman, 1876) closed some years ago. After being briefly used as a museum of the lace industry, it is now the Pitcher & Piano, a highly popular bar. Some may find this use incongruous, but the conversion has preserved the internal form of the building, and the magnificent stained glass by William Morris and Edward Burne-Jones can now be freely viewed any day of the week. The conversion of the former Shire Hall next door as the Galleries of Justice, a project completed in 1998 with Maber Associates as architects, benefited from both Heritage Lottery and EU funding, and allows public access to a building that was previously largely inaccessible. Caruso St John's Centre for Contemporary Art Nottingham (CCAN) is to occupy the adjacent Garners Hill site, forming a new gateway to the Lace Market and infusing a new element of cultural activity into the area.

The Lace Market, which once seemed a symbol of decline, is now a vibrant city quarter, a place to live, and a place for entertainment with bars and restaurants. By commissioning

Julian Marsh for a radical conversion of a derelict Lace Market factory as a pioneering 'eco-house', local member of Parliament Alan Simpson has underlined his own commitment to environmentally conscious design as well as his faith in the Lace Market area itself. The Lace Market Hotel on High Pavement has been such a success, pioneering locally the idea of a 'boutique hotel' or 'town-house hotel', that it recently expanded into 27 High Pavement, where thirteen extra bedrooms have been created. The conversion by Maber Associates, in succession to Cox Freeman, has respected the character of the listed building (which was formerly the County Tavern), while updating it with modern services and giving it an assured future. The project epitomizes the spirit behind the Lace Market today. This is where the story of Nottingham began; now it is a quarter where the past is treasured but not embalmed, where city-centre living has taken off in a remarkable way.

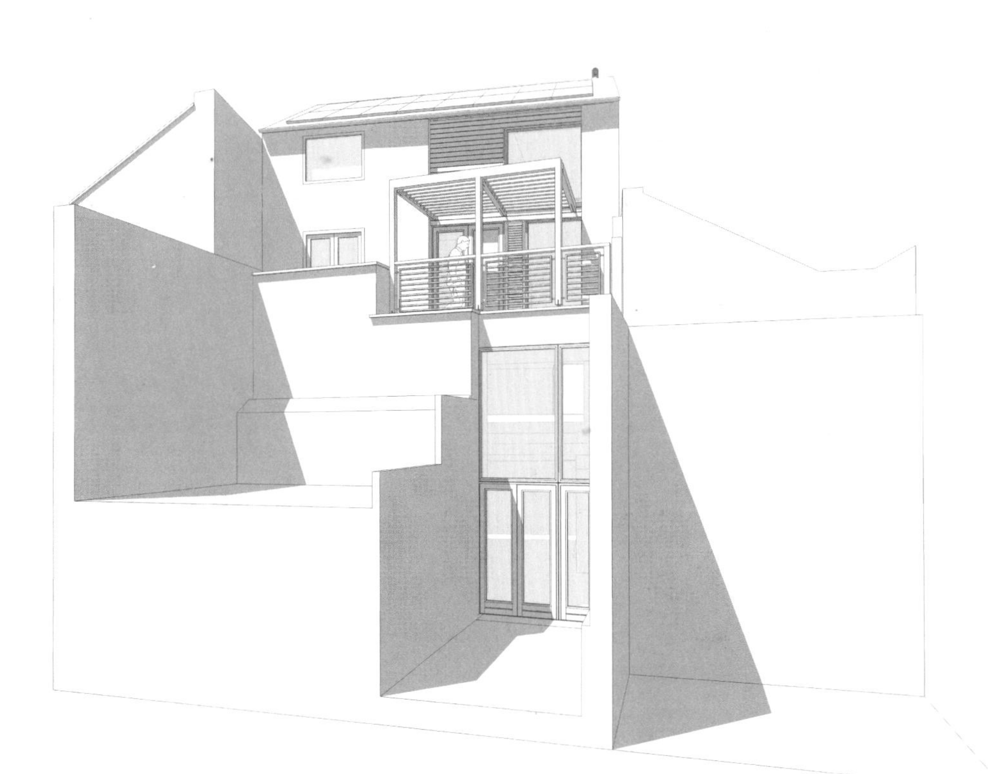

The new Lace Market Square, including apartments, shops and restaurants, provides the area with an attractive public space (above). Alan Simpson's house (right) is designed by Marsh Grochowski on ecological principles.

CASE STUDY

The Adams Building New College

CPMG Architects 1996–98

T.C. Hine's warehouse on Stoney Street, built for Adams and Page and opened in 1855, is the prime monument to Nottingham's lace industry. It was always exceptional, even among the many splendid warehouses of the Lace Market, both for its scale and the range of facilities it provided for those who worked there – a library, canteen and even a chapel. "Even the rear ... has elegance," commented Pevsner. The company closed down in 1950 and the building subsequently passed into multi-occupation, with virtually no investment in maintenance. By the 1970s its deteriorating condition was giving cause for concern, and the building featured prominently in plans to regenerate the Lace Market from the mid-1970s onwards.

The £16.5 million refurbishment of the Adams Building for New College Nottingham (a highly successful further-education college) has given this industrial palazzo an assured future. The project was developed on the basis of a Private Finance Initiative bidding process, with Morrison Construction Group selected as preferred bidder in April 1997, and their architects, CPMG, subsequently commissioned to develop the scheme. Grant aid came from the Heritage Lottery Fund, European Regional Development Fund, and the regeneration agency English Partnerships.

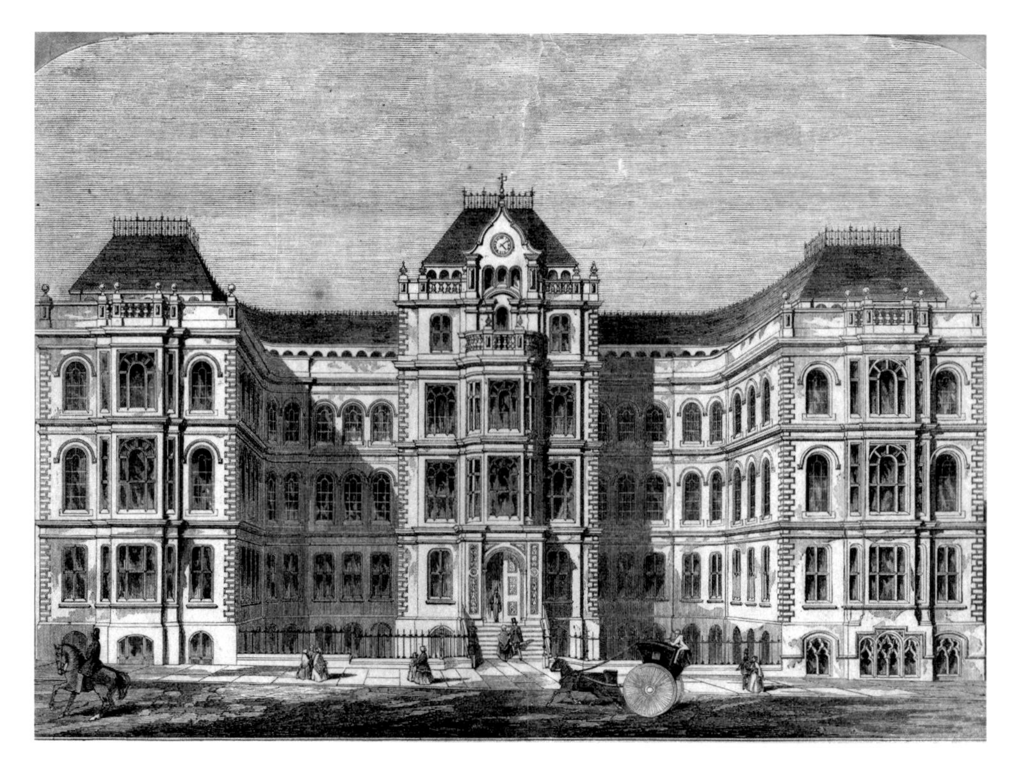

Opened in 1855, the Adams Building designed by T.C. Hine was the flagship of the local lace industry. The restored warehouse (opposite) now houses New College Nottingham.

Former workshop spaces such as this lantern room (right) for fine lacework have adapted well for use as art and design studios (opposite). The Adams Building has imposing frontages on both Stoney Street and St Mary's Gate (below), and will now also face on to Lace Market Square.

On one level, the project was about restoration – cleaning and repairing the fabric of the listed building and removing later accretions, such as the Second World War air-raid shelters that disfigured the Stoney Street frontage. The internal spaces, with their generous head heights, proved highly suitable for the new educational use, and the aim was to minimize new interventions. Where timber floor beams had failed through overloading, for example, they were repaired by laminating new timber on top of the old rather than replaced with new construction. Entirely new services were, of course, essential. To accommodate service ducts, floor levels had to be slightly raised, with the ducts exposed behind perforated metal panels. The aim was to retain the building's industrial character; this was equally reflected in the design of the new steel staircase and the lift ingeniously slotted into a former goods-hoist shaft. The distinctive dual entrance and carriageway were retained and glass doors used to form a new enclosed lobby, providing modern amenity with minimal visual intrusion. The colour scheme used internally is based on the original, with the shades adapted in line with modern taste. In the Victorian period, Thomas Adams's employees enjoyed working conditions that were, by the standards of the time, exceptional. Today the students using the Adams Building have a health spa, restaurant and brasserie, and other leisure facilities that few other city-centre colleges can offer.

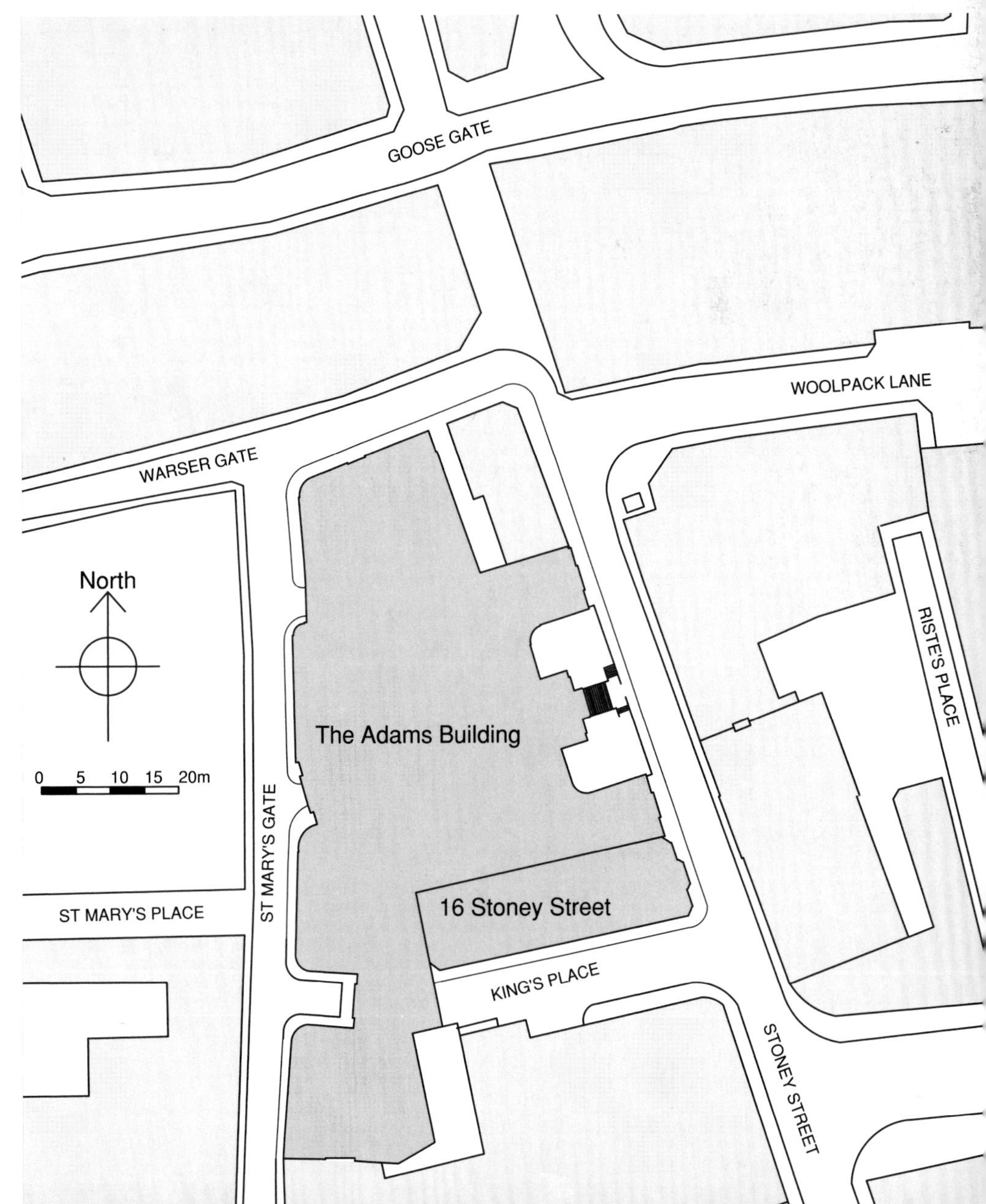

Bottle Lane

Benson + Forsyth
2005–07

The site for Benson + Forsyth's first project in Nottingham lies at a significant node in the city centre, close to the Market Square, metres away from one of the city's principal shopping streets, and on the edge of the Lace Market. The greater part of it has lain derelict for some years, a blot on the city centre. The site owners, Bildurn Properties, wanted to commission a high-quality, distinctive building, and a design competition was held, managed by Derek Latham. Benson + Forsyth, Shed KM, Stanton Williams, HBMA and Rick Mather were shortlisted, and Benson + Forsyth were eventually appointed.

Bottle Lane is a narrow thoroughfare, medieval in origin, extending sharply uphill on an east–west line from Bridlesmithgate to Fletcher Gate, now a principal tram route and the division between the core of the city centre and the distinctive Lace Market and adjacent Hockley quarter to the east. Historically, this was a point of entry to the town from Saxon times on. The narrow King John's Arcade, currently little more than a shabby passageway, extends along the southern edge of the site. The disused tunnel of the Great Central Railway lies below ground and its existence posed a challenge.

The planning brief for the site encouraged the retention of the surviving buildings fronting Fletcher Gate. Number 12 was utterly derelict and considered to have no potential for reuse, but numbers 14 to 16 were in good condition. The scheme that received planning consent in June 2005 retains the front range of these buildings, which will be incorporated into a development that includes a hotel, restaurant and shops. English Heritage opposed the demolition of the other properties on the site, including a neo-Tudor pub of the 1920s, which are within a Conservation Area (though none is listed), though the Commission for Architecture and the Built Environment strongly supported the scheme. English Heritage also objected to the scale of the proposals, though the recently completed apartment development that faces the site across Fletcher Gate is, in fact, taller than the proposed Bottle Lane scheme.

Another important consideration was the protection of important city-centre views, including those of and from the castle and of the tower of the Council House. Computer and physical modelling was used to develop the massing of the scheme in its historic context.

A case might have been made to take the building height established on the east side of Fletcher Gate as the basis for a redevelopment of the west side of the street. Instead, Benson + Forsyth opted for a block that takes its cue, in terms of scale, from adjacent Victorian buildings and accommodates double-height, top-lit arcade space containing shops set behind a glazed screen. The retail block is topped by a garden terrace wrapped around three sides of the hotel and offering good views of the castle and Council House.

The four-storey hotel block rises behind and is a more solid composition, though with striking panoramic windows on the cantilevered south face along Fletcher Gate, which contains a bar and restaurant – likely to be one of the most spectacular modern interiors in the city. The elevation along Bottle Lane is heavily glazed and activated by the lifts and stairs, providing access to the roof terrace (the point of interface between the retail and hotel elements of the scheme) and bar and restaurant located at the junction with Fletcher Gate. At the top of Bottle Lane, this elevation steps down to just two storeys. The hotel reception area is located behind the retained façade of number 16 Fletcher Gate, extending back into a café-bar area along King John's Arcade, bringing new activity to this neglected space. All bedrooms, it is promised, will offer uninterrupted views of the city skyline.

Strongly modelled and with a dramatic presence that recalls, on a smaller scale, the same architects' Museum of Scotland in Edinburgh, the Bottle Lane project is a bold but not insensitive addition to the fabric of the city centre. The fact that architecture of this quality is now commissioned by the commercial sector is a reflection of the steadily rising profile of Nottingham as a city where high-quality new design is no longer a rarity.

Occupying a long-derelict site, the scheme will form a new focal point on Fletcher Gate (above). A model shows how the mass of the scheme is imaginatively broken down (opposite).

Centre for Contemporary Art Nottingham, High Pavement

Caruso St John
2006–08

The Centre for Contemporary Art Nottingham (CCAN) promises to be a facility that is not only innovative in the context of Nottingham's cultural life, but is unique among visual arts institutions in Britain. It has been designed by the highly regarded practice of Caruso St John, which won the project in competition in 2004. The practice is particularly known for its new art gallery in Walsall in the West Midlands.

CCAN aims to bring together conventional 'object-based' art and performance art. The latter has its origins in the New York of the 1960s, and the parallels that the architects draw between Manhattan's SoHo (then the base for avant-garde artists) and Nottingham's Lace Market are not entirely fanciful. The site for CCAN is at the gateway to the Lace Market, where tranquil High Pavement meets the busy highway of Fletcher Gate/Middle Hill. Steeply sloping (the drop from High Pavement to Cliff Road is 13 m/42 ft) and still bearing the scars inflicted by the construction of the Great Central Railway in the 1890s, it incorporates the stepped route of Garners Hill that once led down from the old town to the marshes below. For thirty years, this route has culminated in the bathos of the Broad Marsh Centre, but the centre is to be totally redeveloped and Garners Hill will be reinstated, in widened form, as an attractive pedestrian connection. CCAN will be a pivotal link, helping to repair the fractured townscape between the Lace Market, the Broad Marsh area and the core of the city centre.

The post-competition development of the scheme involved detailed study of broadly comparable venues in Britain and across Europe: London's Camden Arts Centre, the Tramway Art Gallery in Glasgow, the De Pont Foundation for Contemporary Art in Tilburg, The Netherlands, and Peter Zumthor's Kunsthaus in Bregenz, Austria, were seen as particularly relevant models. Practising artists were brought into discussions on the development of the project brief. Flexibility is a fundamental ingredient in the final scheme, with a deliberate attempt to create spaces with the variety of scale, texture and detail found in the converted buildings that so often succeed triumphantly as showcases for contemporary art.

The topography of the site allows the 3120 sq m (33,580 sq ft) building to be conveniently accessed at several levels, and led to a decision to concentrate most of the accommodation on two large floors. The main public entrance to the centre is located in a covered yard at the intersection of High Pavement and Garners Hill. A second entrance is formed on the lower level with access from Middle Hill and Cliff Road, where the café-bar can extend into an open yard, with loading and services access provided at basement level on Cliff Road. Internally, the galleries at the upper level have a 5 m (16 ft) clear height, while the lower exhibition level is a lozenge-shaped space, column-free and deliberately cavernous in character, 8 m (26 ft) high and filling the site. In total, nearly 2000 sq m (21,528 sq ft) of gallery space can be provided. A staircase following the line of Garners Hill connects the two floors, and mezzanine levels extend along the south and west sides of the lower gallery.

The massing of the building, superficially reminiscent of the 'Brutalist' compositions of the 1960s, is actually a response to the exigencies of the site, which was covered with buildings until the Victorian railway builders cleared it. Its modelling is intended to reinforce the powerful topography of the escarpment and to evoke the juxtaposition of masses seen in the historic townscape. The prominent roof lights of cast glass provide markers for the centre from afar. (It is to be topped by a planted roof, attractive to look at from above and providing sound insulation.) The unashamedly tough, industrial quality of the building is offset by the delicately decorative quality of its external surfaces, where coloured, patterned pre-cast concrete is used to recall a memory of the lace on which Nottingham's fortunes were once founded. Large areas of glazing on High Pavement, Middle Hill and Garners Hill emphasize the connection of the building and what goes on inside it with the city. This is no fortress of art, but a place where art seeks to break out of its conventional boundaries.

The Town Hall stood on the site, at the junction of High Pavement and Fletcher Gate (left), until it was cleared for the railway in 1898. The Centre for Contemporary Art steps down from High Pavement towards the Broad Marsh Centre (opposite); its textured façade deliberately recalls Nottingham's famous lace industry.

WATERWAYS
ROBIN
No 1
May B

Canal Corridor

Canal Corridor

Wilford Street and Castle Boulevard in 1927 (left), showing Newcastle House to the left and the British Waterways warehouse to the right. Formerly a central part of the city's industrial base, shown below in the early twentieth century, the canal has now re-emerged as a leisure quarter (opposite).

"It's just like Venice," says Paul Morel to his mother, in D.H. Lawrence's Sons and Lovers (1913), as they walk from Midland Station along Carrington Street, peering down to the canal, busy with barges. The Nottingham Canal opened in 1793, allowing barge traffic from the River Trent to access wharves close to the centre of the town. A few years later it was extended to Langley Mill and Beeston, where it rejoins the Trent. (The Langley Mill branch of the canal was closed in the 1930s and later filled in.) Though soon overtaken by the railways as a means of transporting goods, the canal remained in commercial use into the post-war years, thereafter becoming increasingly a half-forgotten aspect of the city. In the 1950s, as Arthur Seaton, the anti-hero of Alan Sillitoe's novel *Saturday Night and Sunday Morning*, walks in the footsteps of Paul Morel from the Meadows into the city centre, "a wind ascended from low-lying marshalling yards, from swampy canal banks and minnow streams."

By the post-war period, the canal was part of the old industrial city, warts and all. Yet the separation of the city centre from the Trent means that the canal is all the more significant to Nottingham. Like other large British cities, Nottingham began to rediscover its waterfront

WATERWAYS
DIONYSUS
May B'
ROBIN
K. STEWART-HARGREAVES
NOTTINGHAM

The glazed atrium of the Magistrates' Courts opens on to a new public space (opposite). Broadhead's Newcastle House (1932–33, right), a remarkable Modernist building faithfully restored in recent years. A modest but attractive regeneration project, the John A. Stephens Showroom and Warehouse by Marsh Grochowski (below).

in the 1970s, when the first plans for the regeneration of the canal corridor emerged. More immediately, a tidy-up operation made the canal more accessible and more inviting, though its appeal was not yet obvious to property owners and developers.

F.A. Broadhead's Newcastle House (formerly Viyella House) of 1932–33 was saved from demolition by the designation of a Conservation Area around it, and by subsequent listing: the building was significant not only for its stylish Modernist façade, but also for its flat-slab concrete construction. After local entrepreneur Ken Grundy of Bendigo Properties acquired Newcastle House from a London-based property company, it was successfully restored, the brief to James McArtney Architects being to maintain the external form of the building, replacing missing and decayed elements, and to retain its open internal plan while converting it to modern offices. The replication of the concrete panels on the exterior was facilitated by the survival of the original moulds at the Nottingham works of Trent Concrete, which had constructed the building. New glazing was installed on the pattern of the original steel glazing systems, though upgraded to meet modern environmental and safety standards. The reconstruction of the elevation facing the canal was carried out in contemporary style rather than as a reproduction of the style of the 1930s. Internally, partitions and suspended ceilings were kept to a minimum to allow the building's fine structure to be fully appreciated. It was probably the example of Newcastle House that persuaded the Inland Revenue to select a canalside site for its new headquarters; designed by Michael Hopkins, the development set a new standard for office design in Nottingham and won much critical acclaim.

The relatively modest office rents obtainable in Nottingham did not encourage similar ventures from the commercial sector and the availability of other large development sites close to the city centre (the General Hospital and Boots' 'island' site) was equally discouraging. In this light, the regeneration of Castle Wharf, achieved without large subventions of grant aid, was all the more remarkable. Built in two phases, Castle Wharf includes new offices for the *Nottingham Evening Post* along with offices for British Telecom and the NatWest bank. The office buildings are essentially contextual designs, responding to the industrial aesthetic of the canalside with their use of brick and stone with pitched roofs. On a fine evening and at weekends, Castle Wharf is packed with people drawn by the open waterfront and the bars that spill out on to the canal banks. The last of the major canal warehouses to survive has found a successful leisure use after the failure of a museum project based there. Across the canal, the Magistrates' Courts are necessarily less permeable, and their Post-modernist

monumentality already seems dated, though the decision to locate the complex here has undoubtedly added to the liveliness of the area.

Further to the east, financial company Capital One's major investment in new offices, an inspirational mix of rehabilitation and new build close to Midland Station, has extended the process of regeneration by osmosis, as it were. The Eastside project is a potential new city quarter on the former Boots site – no longer an island – progressively cleared during the 1980s and 1990s. The project offers a future for the fine warehouses built by the Great Northern Railway adjacent to the former London Road station. The station itself, a major work of T.C. Hine, downgraded and finally closed by British Rail, was converted, with commendable care for the historic fabric, into a Holmes Place Health Club by Colman Architects in 1998–2001.

The new vitality of the canal corridor has had a knock-on effect on new development along the southern edge of the city centre. Letts Wheeler Architects' excellent Park Rock housing, built on what was derelict land off Castle Boulevard, at the foot of the castle escarpment, represented a daring, but subsequently highly successful, venture for locally based Braemore Properties. In the hinterland of the Inland Revenue, Marsh Grochowski Architects' stylish but economical (£1.4 million) transformation of the John A. Stephens showroom and warehouse on Castle Meadow Road demonstrates the potential for an industrial shed to be something more than a visual disaster. Undertaken by a long-established local business, the project reflects the new pride and confidence in an area of Nottingham which was once regarded as an industrial wasteland.

The former Great Northern (Low-level) Station lay derelict and in need of a new use for many years (opposite right). The building was successfully refurbished in 1998–2001 as the Holmes Place Health Club, with a complete internal and external restoration (opposite far left; above).

CASE STUDY

Inland Revenue Headquarters

Hopkins Architects
1992–95

Michael Hopkins's Inland Revenue headquarters is one of the key late-twentieth-century landmarks of Nottingham. The more than 2000 new jobs that the development brought provided a boost for Nottingham in the aftermath of the 1980s, a decade that had seen the city's manufacturing base shrink, and also launched the regeneration of the neglected canal corridor. But there was a degree of brinkmanship in the planning negotiations that, in the event, ended happily. The government's initial plan, conceived in 1989, was to produce a mundane design-and-build office complex (by Percy Thomas Partnership) on the site. The City Council was unhappy with the proposals, as was the Civic Society, and the then Royal Fine Art Commission stepped in to express "strong opposition to the proposals which, because of their bulk and colour, would have had a serious effect on the nearby castle and reduced its primacy as the city's most prominent monument". The local authority held the line, despite suggestions that the Inland Revenue might abandon the scheme and move elsewhere. In 1991, the government announced that the proposal had been scrapped and that an architectural competition was to be held. Of six schemes shortlisted, including a Gothic proposal by Demetri Porphyrios and a low-energy glazed shed by Richard Rogers, Hopkins's submission was eventually selected. The development, 40,000 sq m (430,560 sq ft) of office space in six blocks, plus an amenity building, was completed in February 1995. It constitutes, in effect, a new urban quarter, its streets open to pedestrians although not to general traffic, which has played an important role in the rediscovery of the canalside as a new asset for everyone.

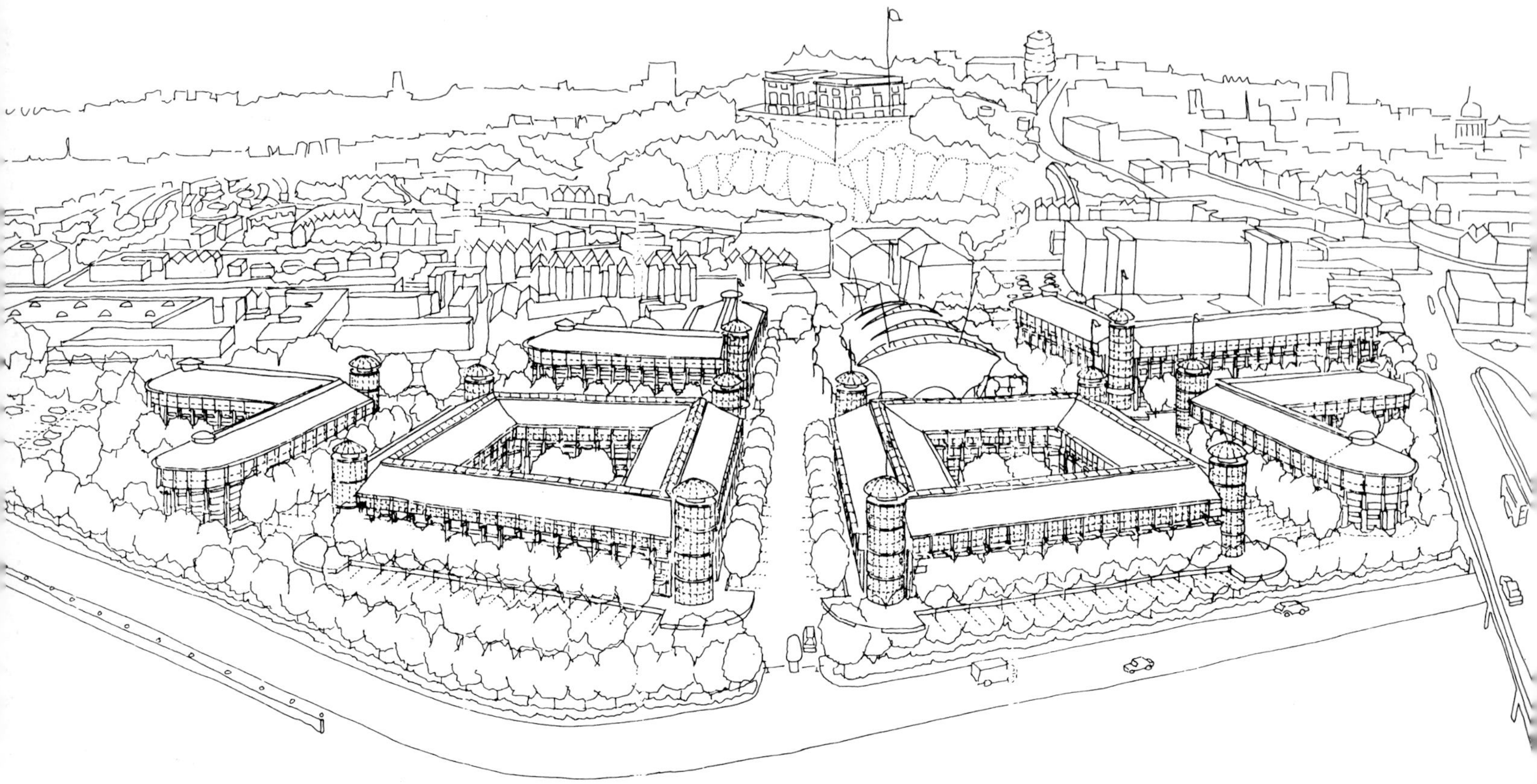

The project has created a new urban quarter (below), complete with streets, rather than an enclosed office precinct. The layout of the project is designed to protect and enhance views of the castle, with the suggestion of city walls and gates in the stair towers influenced by the castle's military architecture (opposite).

Inland
Revenue

The mix of materials – red brick, steel and glass – refers to the local vernacular (left). The masted tensile structure at the centre of the complex houses the staff restaurant and other facilities and has a jaunty recreational air (opposite).

Like the later Jubilee Campus at the University of Nottingham, the Inland Revenue Headquarters made extensive use of prefabrication and standardized components to secure economy (a budget of £50 million was set) and speed of construction – the Inland Revenue had to rent a number of buildings in the city as it waited for its new base to be completed. The use of brick, not a new material for Hopkins, suggested a sympathy for the established local industrial vernacular, although it was employed not as a cladding, but as a key structural component. This is, indeed, a project in which architecture, structure and environmental design are integrated – the need for low running costs, with natural light and ventilation used as far as possible, was an important element of the competition brief. The six buildings, four of them L-shaped and two larger blocks with central courtyards, were designed for potential letting should the space requirements of the Inland Revenue change. The Hopkins proposal responded perfectly to this provision.

Stout brick piers, using a hard brick of characteristically local dimensions but fabricated off-site, support the floors of the office buildings (typically 13.6 m/44 ft wide), which are formed of pre-cast concrete slabs that are attached via the concrete caps to the piers. Attic storeys are lightweight structures of steel and glass into which the lead-covered roofs of the office buildings are integrated. Circular stair towers of glass brick in steel frames are set at the corner of each building – they are much more than rhetorical gestures, acting as thermal chimneys to exhaust stale air from the buildings. The 'green' aspirations of the project were serious, and are reflected in external shading, plentiful insulation, opening

windows and, of course, the use of heavy-weight materials that provide thermal mass and counter the effects of the external environment, whether the weather is especially hot or cold. Exposed concrete barrel vaults are a distinctive feature of the office spaces, and provide a convenient location for lights and other services. The buildings have an honesty and straightforwardness that genuinely evoke the 'functional tradition' of industrial design and, though there have been problems with the operation of the low-energy ventilation system, the scheme was a brave and pioneering exercise in 'green' design from which many lessons have been learned.

For the amenity building, with its restaurant, bar, crèche and sports facilities, the Hopkins team used a tensile fabric structure, a lightweight technology that had become a hallmark of Hopkins's work, for example at the Glyndebourne Opera House in East Sussex and Lord's Cricket Ground in London. The great tent is hung from four big masts that are distinctive markers in the townscape. It is in its urban contribution, in fact, that the scheme gives most to the city. Eschewing strict Modernist urban formulae, Hopkins places the buildings around tree-lined streets that focus on the castle, set high above on its rock. Limited parking for employees' cars is provided on the streets, rather than in costly basements or a separate building. As a humane and highly practical approach to the design of a bureaucratic compound, this project takes some beating. Anyone who wants to see the antithesis is recommended to visit the city of Leeds, where the design-and-build Department of Health headquarters, a product of the same process of civil-service devolution, is a monolithic blot on the landscape.

CASE STUDY

Castle Wharf

Franklin Ellis Architects 1996–99

A mix of refurbishment and new build, the Castle Wharf project was a key component in the regeneration of the canal corridor, itself one of the landmark achievements in the transformation of the city centre. The completion in 1995 of the new Inland Revenue headquarters on a large site between the canal and railway, followed by the opening of the Magistrates' Courts on land just across the canal from what became Castle Wharf, provided an irresistible catalyst for the development of the site. The City Council was anxious to see a mixed-use scheme in tune with the character of the Conservation Area, with important views of the castle from the canal towpath and Carrington Street protected. Though it was judged that a number of the existing buildings on the site could be replaced, the Grade II-listed British Waterways warehouse was recognized as a landmark that had to find a suitable new use. In the development of an aesthetic for the new buildings on the site, the predominant theme was that of context rather than the creation of iconic landmarks. Red brick was generally used as a facing material, reinforcing the existing character of the canalside.

In terms of uses, offices would form the foundation of the scheme, with around 11,150 sq m (120,000 sq ft) of flexible space. The development was enterprisingly undertaken by local developers, Monk Sowden, and followed a limited-invitation architectural competition. The scheme was underwritten by the commitment of a group of core tenants: the *Nottingham Evening Post* (relocating from the site of what subsequently became the Cornerhouse), British Telecom (BT) and the NatWest bank, with buildings developed in line with their specific requirements. There was also a clear opportunity to develop leisure facilities, bars, pubs and restaurants along the waterfront, amounting to around 2787 sq m (30,000 sq ft) of space. The listed warehouse had particular potential for leisure use, with a new boardwalk created along the canal providing a connection from Wilford Street through to a new public square at the core of the site, where a new two-storey pub was developed (thus blocking out noise from Canal Street to the north).

The office buildings (all four storeys in height) share a common basic vocabulary but have been tailored to the specific needs of their occupants. The *Nottingham Evening Post* building, for example, is seen as a 'gateway' on the approach to the city centre along Wilford Street from the south, and features a bold sweep of glazing as a focal point. BT's building focuses on a central, full-height atrium, containing a staff restaurant, that is visible from the exterior and further animates the site.

British Waterways played an important role, releasing land, promoting canalside activities and most importantly renovating the run-down warehouse that towered over the site.

The success of this scheme depends less on its architecture than on its handling of public space, with the creation of legible north–south and east–west pedestrian routes through the site a key feature. Of a fine evening or weekend Castle Wharf is packed with people enjoying the waterfront on which Nottingham had for so long turned its back.

The Castle Wharf project was a key element in the regeneration of Nottingham's canalside. The area is now a successful commercial district by day and a vibrant leisure quarter by night.

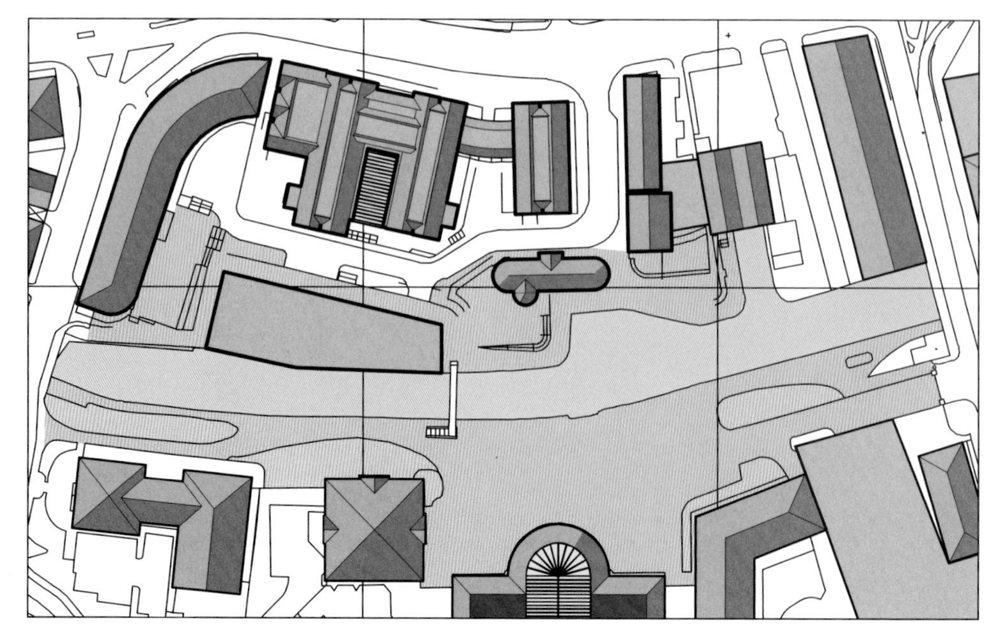

BRITISH
WATERWAYS

CASE STUDY

Park Rock, Castle Boulevard

Letts Wheeler Architects
2003–04

The site of Letts Wheeler's Park Rock housing scheme has a fascinating history. Located at the base of the sandstone escarpment on which the castle stands, it was occupied for centuries by Lenton Hermitage, supposedly created by monks from Lenton Priory, with cells and a chapel dug into the rock, and the River Leen (culverted during the nineteenth century) running along its southern perimeter. The caves (scheduled as an Ancient Monument) survived every transformation of the surrounding area, and were used as air-raid shelters during the Second World War, but by the 1990s the site was a derelict eyesore, used for flytipping and other antisocial activities, contaminated with petrol and chemicals, and partly occupied by run-down sheds. The only future for it seemed to be low-grade commercial development, which would have been an unfortunate outcome in view of the remarkable regeneration of the nearby canal corridor and the proximity of the salubrious villa-lined avenues of the Park to the north.

Thanks to Nottingham-based architects Letts Wheeler, however, the potential of the site was unlocked to create an outstanding residential development, close to the city centre, that makes reference to the typology of the Victorian villa in an entirely contemporary manner. Letts Wheeler approached local developer Braemore Properties with their ideas for the site, which Braemore promptly acquired, progressing the scheme to planning consent in tandem with the architects. The protected status of the caves necessitated detailed consultation with English Heritage and other bodies as well as city planners, and a key element of the scheme was to be the restoration of public access to the site. Views of the site from Castle Boulevard were to be retained, so that the development, containing thirty-eight apartments, was broken down into a series of six blocks placed directly on the street, away from the escarpment, separated by large paved courtyards, so that the cave entrances can be glimpsed from the Boulevard. They are illuminated by night, and part of the romantic Victorian landscape that once existed around them has been recreated as an amenity for residents.

This refreshingly sophisticated scheme takes an enterprising approach to the dramatic site on the edge of the Castle escarpment, with apartment blocks conceived and arranged like Victorian villas on the boulevard and freer in form behind.

Although the 'villa' form of the blocks relates to the nineteenth-century houses that survive in the vicinity, the use of red brick, with steel-framed balconies, and the spare details also suggest an affinity with the 'functional tradition' of the industrial buildings along the canal. Most of the apartments, ranging in size from one to three bedrooms, are duplex units, so that all residents enjoy good views out. Eight units were designed as 'live/work' spaces, with dedicated workspaces at ground-floor level and the potential for business entrances at street level. The highly ordered street elevations are in contrast with those to the side and rear of the apartment blocks, which are more informal.

This is a project that shows an understanding of and respect for historic character and context, yet provides an attractive habitat for a new generation of city dwellers. It exemplifies the way in which the regeneration process can enhance the face of the city.

The circulation space (top) and the cleverly worked space inside an apartment showing the duplex form (above). The frontage of the development (opposite) gives no hint of the dramatic rockscape at the back.

PARKROCK TWO

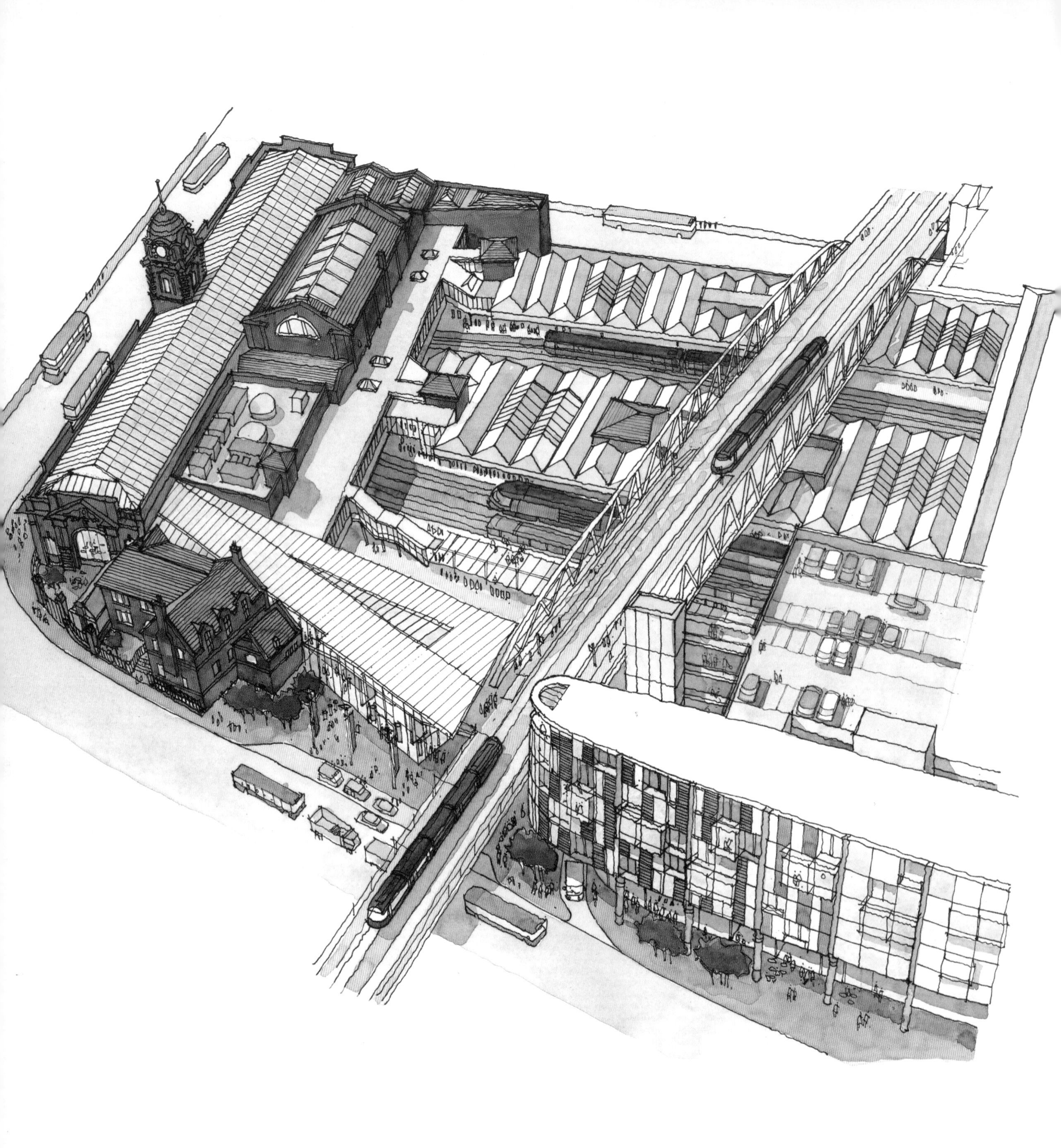

Midland Station regeneration

Building Design Partnership 2005–11

The closure in the 1960s of Victoria Station left the city with only one principal railway station, while severing routes that today could be of great value in improving public transport provision in Nottingham. A paucity of train services apart, Midland Station suffers from its relative isolation from the city centre – exacerbated by the position of the Broad Marsh Centre – and in recent years has become an increasingly shabby and lacklustre gateway to the city.

The redevelopment of the Broad Marsh Centre, regeneration of the canal corridor and the emergence of the Southside quarter of the city (and the Meadows and Waterside beyond) as a dynamic new growth point – new office, hotel and residential developments are already proceeding – underlines the need for investment in the station. The nearby thirteen-storey Jurys Hotel, for example, though architecturally unremarkable, is the largest hotel in the East Midlands. Adjacent office development will total more than 32,520 sq m (350,000 sq ft) of space. The development of the former Hicking Pentecost site, off London Road, includes 329 new flats in the converted factory. Other developments are in the pipeline. The masterplan developed by Building Design Partnership (BDP) in association with the City Council (which does not, of course, own or control the station) aims to deliver "a world-class transport interchange and new business hub for the city". Work on the station itself would partly be restoration of the listed fabric; in the 1980s, for example, British Rail crudely replaced all the glazed platform canopies. There is scope to convert sympathetically the present covered carriage road to contain shops, cafés, a new travel centre and other facilities, as well as to restore the existing concourse and remove inappropriate later accretions.

More radically, it is proposed to develop a new concourse along the southern side of the station, along with a 1000-space multi-storey car park and associated retail and office development, which could help to make the project financially viable. Closer integration of mainline rail services with the expanding NET (Nottingham Express Transit) tram network, with new lines proposed to Clifton and Beeston, is vital. Although the multiplicity of interested parties (including train operators, Network Rail and the Strategic Rail Authority) and uncertainties over the future management of the station continue to pose serious problems, there is a clear commitment from the City Council, along with the County Council and East Midlands Development Agency, to progress the project.

The development includes new offices and other uses on adjacent land and the conversion of the covered carriage road to provide an improved public concourse with shops and restaurants, as well as the restoration of the listed Edwardian station building as the centre of the new transport hub.

City of Business

City of Business

Player's Tobacco was once one of Nottingham's largest employers with a huge factory complex at Radford. The main building (above), once an important symbol of the firm in the city, is now demolished, but parts of the complex still exist. Boots' D10 factory at Beeston was one of the most radical British industrial buildings of the 1930s (opposite).

For two centuries, indeed well into the post-war era, Nottingham's predominant identity was that of a manufacturing town. During the nineteenth century, a specific architecture of industry emerged, generated principally by the practical demands of production, but on occasion – and most obviously in the elaborate warehouses of the Lace Market – by motives of self-advertisement and display.

The "new" industries that came to dominate the local scene by the early decades of the twentieth century – tobacco, pharmaceuticals and bicycles – all developed an architectural expression of their own. Some of Player's factories in Radford, now demolished, were highly impressive. Raleigh Cycle's headquarters on Lenton Boulevard, which survives in new use, was designed by T.C. Howitt (who also worked for the Home Ales Brewery). But above all it was the Boots Company, a name that became synonymous with Nottingham, which emerged as an outstanding patron of architecture. As a retailer, Boots had an obvious interest in display and the flagship store on High Street that Jesse Boot commissioned from architect A.N. Bromley remains (it is now a fashion store) a much-admired feature of the city centre. Boots' move to Beeston, generated by the sheer need for space in order to expand (though it retained a major city-centre presence until relatively recently) led to the commissioning of the city's greatest industrial landmarks. Owen Williams's two great factory buildings at Beeston, constructed between 1930 and 1938, reflected the architect's aim to achieve "fitness of purpose at minimum cost in a combination with complete flexibility for replanning and alteration". The agenda was practical, but the aesthetics, if incidental to the project, won enthusiastic approval from Modernist critics: "a building that our century can be proud of", Anthony Bertram wrote in 1938 of the D10 building.

Boots remains an institution, but its business has changed with the times, and both D10 and the later D6 have been significantly reconfigured as a result. Their status as Grade I-listed buildings meant that proposed changes were intensively scrutinized by English Heritage as well as by local planners. One of Boots' redundant city-centre buildings, the former printing plant on Station Street (a fine structure of the 1950s by the company's in-house architects), has been successfully adapted by Capital One, a credit-card company that is one of the leaders of the city's ongoing business renaissance. Capital One's Loxley House, designed by ORMS, is neatly linked to the refurbished printing plant and is itself one of Nottingham's outstanding new commercial buildings, adopting a progressive approach to the design of interactive working spaces. Another of the business leaders of twenty-first-century Nottingham, the information business Experian, commissioned a leading practice in the field of office architecture, Sheppard Robson, to design its two new buildings in Nottingham, the Landmark House headquarters and the data centre at Ruddington, Experian Fairham House. Both are state-of-the-art commercial buildings that contribute to the public realm while meeting the demanding practical brief imposed by the client.

Capital One and Experian chose to commission their own buildings, fine-tuned to their requirements, rather than to adapt speculatively built office space. Unfortunately much of the latter commodity built in Nottingham in recent years is as disappointing in its way as the worst products of the 1960s, now so generally despised. The Ruddington data centre, for example, has as its neighbours a

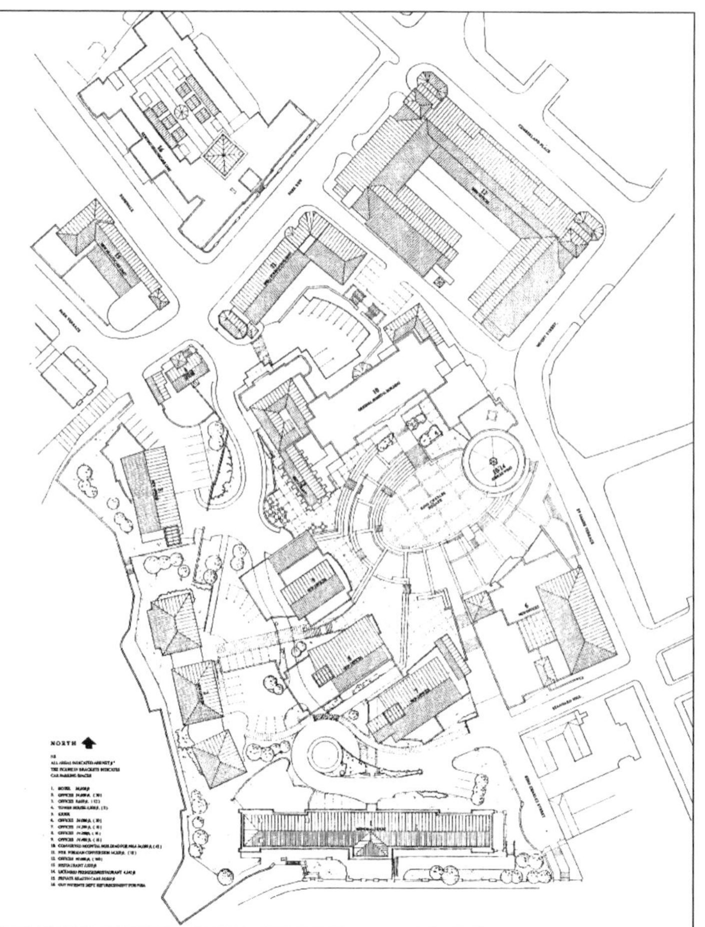

Boots D6 (top) was as radical as the slightly earlier D10, though superficially more conventional. The General Hospital has been transformed (above left and right), keeping the best of the Georgian and Victorian buildings.

number of uninspiring brick-clad blocks that are all too typical of recent business-park architecture. By contrast, the redevelopment of the former General Hospital site on Standard Hill as a mixed-use urban quarter has made a positive contribution to the renaissance of the city centre. One of the benefits of the scheme was the demolition of a bulky 1960s block (Trent Wing) that had a most unfortunate effect on distant views of the castle. As part of the redevelopment of the site, CPMG Architects refurbished the hospital's original building and the Waterhouse Jubilee Wing as headquarters for the Nottingham Health Authority and built a substantial new block, in keeping with its context, as offices for solicitors Eversheds. Though the public spaces provided as part of the project are disappointing (and underused), it has brought enormous benefits to the city and capital gains to the health sector for reinvestment elsewhere.

For the near future, it is to major expansions of the city centre, notably the Eastside project, that one looks for evidence of Nottingham's dynamism as a business centre. In the longer term, the inexorable pressure for redevelopment will, it is hoped, permit the demolition of some of the worst failures of the 1960s and 1970s.

The New Horizon factory (top) was constructed for Player's during the early 1970s. Boots' D90 building (above) was designed in the Miesian manner by US practice Skidmore, Owings & Merrill.

CASE STUDY

Boots D10 Refurbishment Beeston

AMEC
1991–94

Owen Williams's "crystal palace of industry", the Boots 'Wets' factory, was opened in July 1933, with Lady Trent ceremonially smashing a bottle of eau de cologne in place of the more usual champagne. Boots was already a national institution, having just opened its thousandth shop, and D10 was a landmark in its history, described in its publicity material as a "wonder factory" for a new age, costing £300,000, staffed by 1200 workers and with nearly 65,000 sq m (700,000 sq ft) of production and packing space. The building was designed in close collaboration with the client, and at its heart were the great manufacturing and packing halls. (Williams's original design provided for a structure three times as large as that built, including space for the 'Drys' subsequently accommodated in the separate D6 building.) The splendid full-height packing hall, 182 m long and 23 m high (600 x 76 ft), is one of the great British interiors of the twentieth century, roofed in steel and naturally lit by thousands of glass discs set in concrete. Dispensing with conventional walls, Williams clad the exterior of D10 with patent glazing set between the cantilevered reinforced concrete floor slabs. The exposure of the latter led to problems of spalling, though generally the building was in reasonable condition when the company began to consider a refurbishment in the late 1980s.

The refurbishment project, commissioned from AMEC, was concerned with both the restoration of the historic fabric and the creation of new office and laboratory spaces within the building. Building services had to be comprehensively renewed and environmental systems upgraded. Following English Heritage approval (the building is Grade I listed), work started on site in April 1992 and was completed just over two years later, at a cost of around £20 million. During this time the production facilities within the building had be kept running.

Interior view of the D10 building (opposite), showing the enormous manufacturing halls at the heart of the complex. External and interior views (right) when new. The building remains substantially unchanged today.

The most conspicuous change, and one that was potentially controversial, was the complete replacement of 3345 sq m (36,000 sq ft) of external glazing that did not meet the demanding modern standards of energy performance and environmental control. They leaked heat from inside the building in winter and failed to baffle solar gain in summer. On the western elevation, rainwater was penetrating the building. The new double-glazed units were made by Crittall Windows, the manufacturer of the original glazing system, fitted with internal blinds and gently tinted. Sill members have been redetailed to throw off rainwater. The effect of the tinting and the smoothness of the modern glass has undoubtedly changed the appearance of the building, yet the practical case for a new form of glazing was formidable. Equally inevitable was the piercing of Williams's concrete floors, which are 25 cm (10 in) thick, for the installation of new service ducts. The front of the building is now devoted to air-conditioned offices, with raised floors, while new laboratories occupy the ground floor. The greater part of the building, however, fulfils the function for which it was designed; long may it continue to do so.

In 1994–96 Boots teamed up again with AMEC to refurbish the adjacent D6 building (the 'Drys') at a cost of £15 million. The building was only partly in use before rehabilitation and has been partially converted to offices for Boots Healthcare International; former manufacturing and storage spaces have provided spacious, well-lit office areas.

The refurbishment, which involved the renewal of the external skin of the building to meet modern environmental standards (above) also included the insertion of new laboratories at ground-floor level (opposite).

Boots D90 Refurbishment and Extension, Beeston

DEGW
1995–2000

The Boots D90 building when new in 1968 (left). It reflected the strong North American influence on corporate office design at the time. Floor plan, showing the original D90 Building (below left) and the new extension.

Boots' continuing commitment to fine architecture was demonstrated in the 1960s with the commissioning of a new headquarters building at Beeston designed by the American practice of Skidmore, Owings & Merrill (SOM) under Bruce Graham, in association with leading British practice YRM. According to Elain Harwood of English Heritage, the plan derives from Mies van der Rohe's unexecuted 1957 scheme for the Bacardi headquarters in Cuba, which had a central landscaped courtyard as its focus. D90 (now D90 West) was completed in 1968. Its internal fit-out, designed by YRM, was pioneeringly (for 1960s Britain) open plan, with office spaces defined by flexible timber units rather than walls. The building was listed Grade II* in 1996.

DEGW was appointed in 1995 to masterplan the expansion of D90 (20,000 sq m/215,300 sq ft in area) into a 42,000 sq m (450,000 sq ft) head-office complex, accommodating around 2700 staff and allowing the company to vacate a number of buildings it still occupied in central Nottingham. But the aspirations of the £35 million project were not only spatial. Boots wanted to introduce new

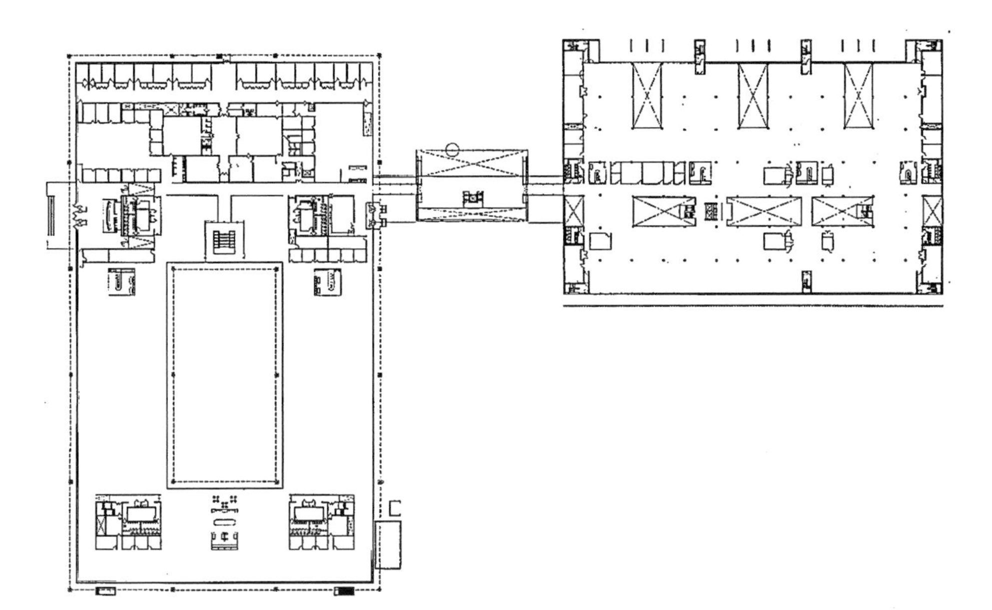

The block that links the extension with the original building is designed in a minimalist style in sympathy with the older architecture (top). The extension (bottom) is an entirely modern and interactive office development.

When opened, the D90 Building (left) was at the leading edge of office design in Britain, taking its cue from North American models. The refurbishment has modernized the office facilities (above) while preserving the building's essential character. DEGW's addition is focused on the central atrium and reflects state-of-the-art thinking about interactive office design (opposite).

ways of working, encouraging interaction between departments and breaking down traditional hierarchies now seen as irrelevant to the business. DEGW, under office design specialist Frank Duffy, was supremely well equipped to bring Boots into the age of ideas exchange, team working, 'neighbourhoods' and 'home bases'. The aspiration promoted by Boots' managing director Steve Russell was nothing less than a new culture of the workplace. Enclosed personal spaces would be greatly reduced, and meeting spaces, many of them informal, multiplied. There was also an aim to provide first-class staff facilities in the best Boots tradition: in a developing local economy, Boots had to compete for the best staff.

The listing of the SOM/YRM building meant that English Heritage had to approve any changes to the fabric, including the built-in furniture and services. A specimen area of the original partitioning was retained, but the rest of the interior has been converted into open-plan space in the twenty-first-century sense of the term, fully equipped with a raised floor for electronic services. Even the managing director has abandoned his private office in favour of a desk in open-plan space.

The greatest challenge was to ensure that the two buildings, D90 West and the new 22,400 sq m (241,100 sq ft) D90 East, functioned in harmony. They are connected by a linking entrance block, a sheer glazed pavilion of great elegance in the best Miesian mould. The two buildings form a working 'village', connected by an internal street that extends through the new building, across the link block and into the original D90. There is a café at each end and meeting spaces everywhere, slickly furnished, as well as areas where you can plug in your laptop and work away. Colour coding identifies the working 'hubs' on each floor of the new block, areas where copying and printing facilities are located alongside coffee points: just the place for that chance conversation that could generate a brilliant new idea. The interior of the building benefits from generous natural light channelled via full-height atria. The central atrium is very much a place to see and be seen: some senior staff reportedly work from the café, ensuring that they see all the colleagues with whom they need to make contact.

The D90 project was driven by a new philosophy of office working, in the same way that Owen Williams's work for Boots in the 1930s was driven by new production techniques. By the 1990s, however, the company had to work within the constraints of the 'heritage' – the diagram of the extension, carefully detached from the listed building, reflects the need to protect the distinct identity of the latter. Yet the project can equally be seen as a success story for the post-war listing programme: SOM's building had to be upgraded and the need for change was conceded. It remains a masterpiece of its era, while the new link block and D90 East manage to be simultaneously both contextual and yet equally credible examples of contemporary design.

CASE STUDY

Capital One Headquarters

DEGW/ORMS

1997–2002

Capital One, with its roots in the US, is now one of the UK's fastest-growing issuers of credit cards, and has become a leading component in the new, increasingly post-industrial economy of twenty-first-century Nottingham. The company's headquarters is located immediately to the north of Midland Station: the choice of a central location, served by public transport (the tram was on its way when the site was chosen), rather than an out-of-town business park dependent on the car, is significant in itself. The project has contributed significantly to the prosperity and liveliness of the city centre: nearly 2500 people now work for Capital One in Nottingham.

Capital One came to Nottingham, a company spokesman commented, "because of the people": the city could provide the able, motivated workforce the company needed. (Only a small number of people are employed at its other UK office, in central London.) Having secured suitably qualified staff and trained them, the company wanted to retain their services.

The aim was to create a high-quality working environment of international standard. The first phase of the project (1997–2000) involved the conversion of the disused Boots printing plant (now Trent House) between Station Street and the canal. The 1950s building was superficially in a poor state, but its handsome Portland stone façade concealed a stout reinforced concrete structure and highly functional and adaptable interiors, essentially industrial in character and principally arranged on two vast (3700 sq m/ 40,000 sq ft) floor levels. DEGW, with its considerable experience of workplace design across the world and pioneering interest in conversion and reuse, was an obvious choice for this phase of the scheme, which needed to accommodate call-centre, restaurant, conference, training and recruitment facilities and support spaces. The telephone call centre occupies the column-free first floor of the building, with its north roof lights providing controlled daylight. The ground floor, with its impressive mushroom columns (reminiscent of Frank Lloyd Wright's famous Johnson Wax offices of 1936–39), contains a mix of offices and support spaces, including the staff restaurant. DEGW's approach has been to conceive of the very large interior spaces as 'townscapes', broken down into identifiable neighbourhoods, linked by 'streets' and animated by landmarks. The structure of the building has been allowed, as much as possible, to speak for itself, with no

Now a major employer in Nottingham, Capital One converted the 1950s Boots Printing Plant to house modern call-centre, office and support facilities.

LEARNING ZONE

attempt to veneer over it. The fit-out is conceived as a freestanding layer within the spaces.

When Capital One first came to Nottingham, it envisaged occupying no more than 4,650 sq m (50,000 sq ft) of space on the Station Street site. It soon realized that much more was needed, especially since it was occupying buildings elsewhere in the city and wanted all its activities in one place. Planning permission for Loxley House, a new £32 million building on Station Street designed by ORMS, was granted in March 2000. It provides an impressive front door to the Capital One complex, externally complementing the older building in terms of scale and materials. The internal layout is custom-designed to reflect the client's commitment to innovative working practices, including a stress on interaction, discussion and the exchange of ideas. In consequence, the office space is largely open plan, with moveable workstations and 20% of the total floor space devoted to meeting rooms, break-out areas and coffee points. Such cellular offices as exist are located at the centre of the floor plates rather than at the edge, leaving access to views and natural light open to all.

The full-height atrium is the operational heart of the place: a secret heart, set apart from the reception area but overlooked by all the office floors, generating a sense of community and activity yet with a sense of calm and order that pervades the building. It is one of the most spectacular modern interiors in Nottingham.

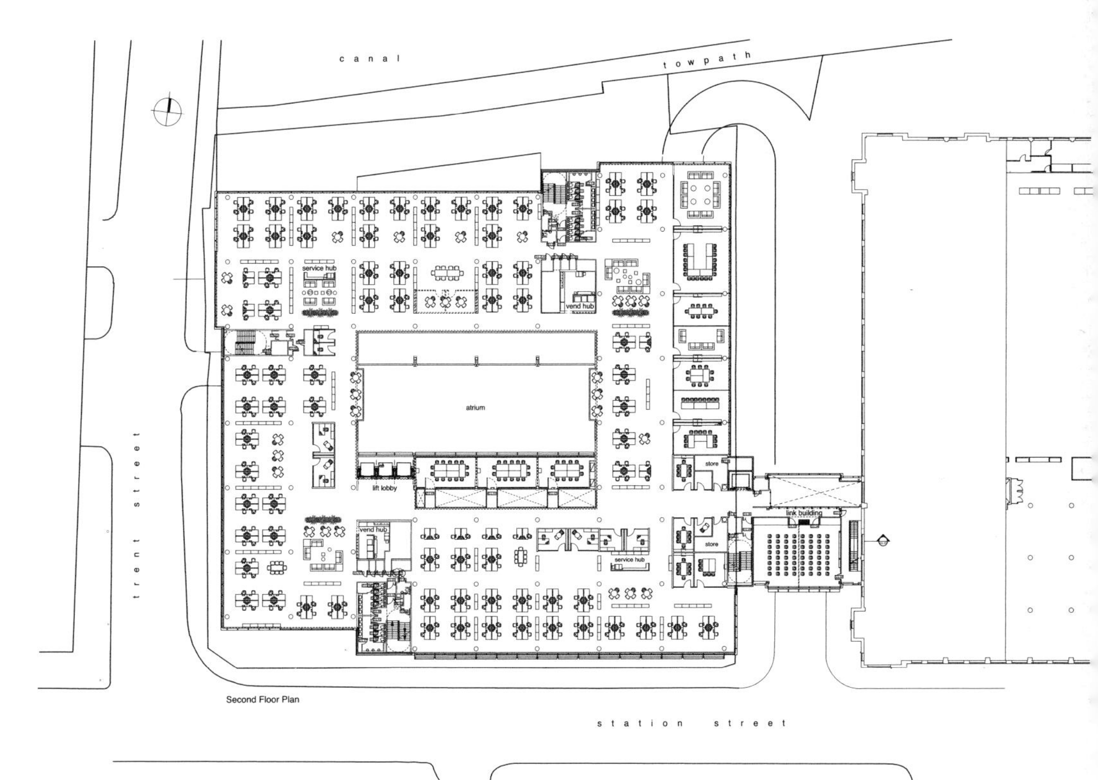

Loxley House, designed by ORMS, is a prestige headquarters building designed around a dramatic central atrium and connected to the converted 1950s building next door.

CASE STUDY

Experian Fairham House Ruddington Fields Business Park Experian Landmark House ng² Business Park Queen's Drive

Sheppard Robson 2000–04

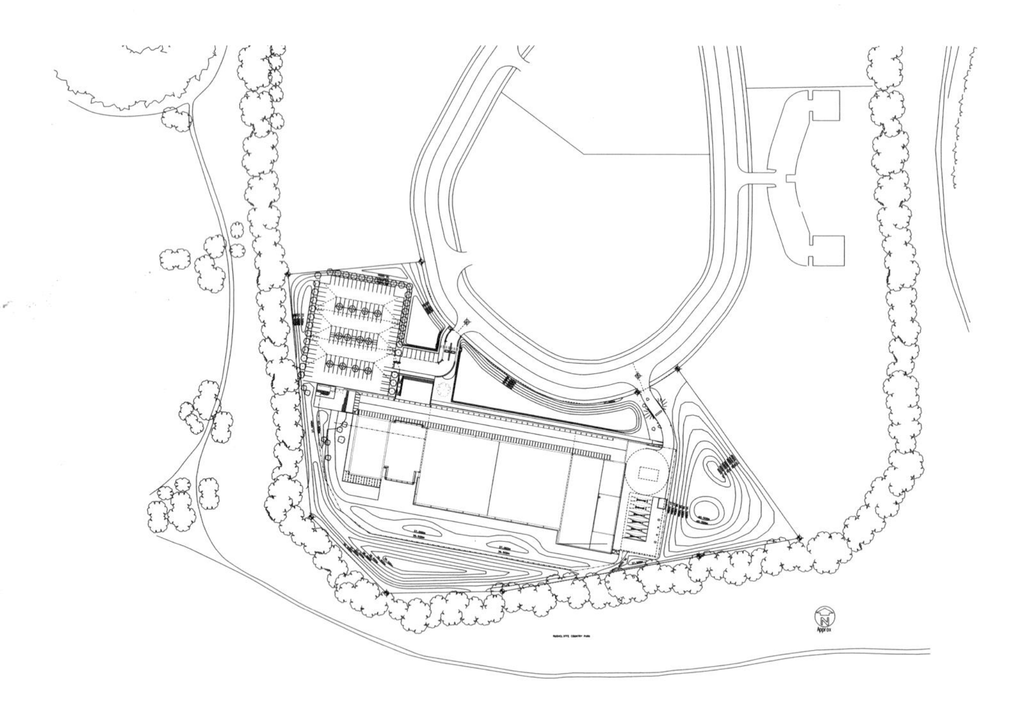

Nottingham has a notable record of inspired business sponsorship of good architecture. In the past, the patrons were prominent individuals, such as Thomas Adams and Jesse Boot. Large twenty-first-century businesses are national, if not global, in character, corporate bodies with less obvious local loyalties. In this context, Experian's commission to Sheppard Robson to design two new buildings in the Nottingham area reflects a welcome commitment to quality design and a belief that good design is good for business.

Experian, part of GUS plc, operates in twenty-two countries and is a multi-billion-pound information business servicing financial institutions worldwide. It now employs over 3000 people in the Nottingham area. The data centre at Ruddington (in a business park developed on the site of the former ordnance depot) was constructed and occupied in little more than a year (2002–03), following planning approval from Rushcliffe Council in March 2002. Planning restrictions limit all buildings on the site to two storeys; most are of a conventional form, with brick cladding commonly used. Experian's data centre stands apart, reflecting the company's concern to commission a building expressive of its business aspirations, and providing excellent working conditions for the skilled staff for which it competes with other businesses in the region.

One fundamental element in the brief for the £20 million building – security and resilience – is clearly legible in its public face. The main elevation, 170 m (560 ft) long, is constructed of weighty pre-cast concrete units, with only narrow window openings apart from the fully glazed entrance pavilion. Behind is an impressive top-lit internal 'street', 150 m (490 ft) long, which connects the linear spaces of the reception area, café, WCs, general offices, meeting rooms and break-out spaces, and provides easy orientation within the building. The real heart of the place is behind. It includes the large network rooms, serviced by large areas of plant, that store the data – these are really highly flexible, column-free steel-framed sheds – and the highly secure 'command bridge', the 'engine room' of the building, deliberately placed at the centre of the complex. The main technical office, accommodating around sixty staff, is placed immediately to the west, where it benefits from good views out to the surrounding countryside. There is scope for the data storage and technical spaces to be expanded by up to 50% without significant disruption to the operation of the facility.

Experian's Data Centre at Ruddington is a highly secure and sophisticated information storage facility, set behind a 170 m (560 ft) concrete façade and protected by a moat.

Experian's headquarters building, Landmark House, is designed for creative interaction with the social space of the central atrium at its heart. It features a cantilevered pod which houses the main entrance to the building with meeting and conference rooms and makes effective use of coloured glass (opposite).

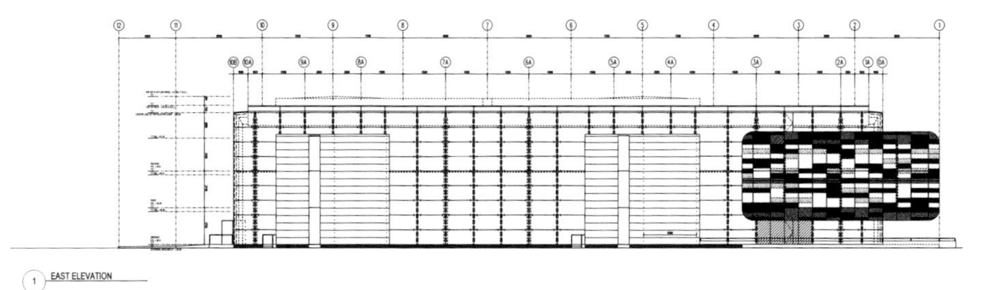

Experian's Landmark House occupies a plot in the ng² Business Park (also developed on a former military site) and was constructed in thirteen months, between August 2003 and September 2004, at a cost of £13.5 million. (A second phase is projected, bringing the total investment to £25 million.) Landmark House has a function very different from that of the Ruddington data centre – it is an administrative headquarters accommodating up to 750 staff relocated from a number of buildings in the city – but there are similarities in the diagram of the two buildings. At Landmark House Sheppard Robson reused the internal 'street' form to create an open, transparent, interactive zone, with a restaurant and shop, that marks the transition from public to private space. This is a place for informal meetings and the chance encounters seen, in the current philosophy of workplace design, as vital to creative thinking 'outside the box'. Stairs and WCs are located in projecting cores. A two-storey cantilevered pod forms the most distinctive element of the building's exterior, housing the main entrance to the building with enclosed meeting and conference rooms above. The use of panels of blue glass, varying in hue and set to a random pattern in a double-layered façade, makes this feature a beacon for the development, especially after dark. Office areas are contained in three-storey wings 15 m (50 ft) wide, extending at right angles to the 'street'. For all its glossy looks, the building is extremely energy-efficient, with the use of chilled beams to cool the office areas and natural stack ventilation in the 'street'. This is a landmark building that gives Experian a strong visual identity, but it is also a highly practical, high-value investment, as the Adams Building and Boots D10 were in their day.

Eastside Masterplan

Hopkins Architects
2002–10

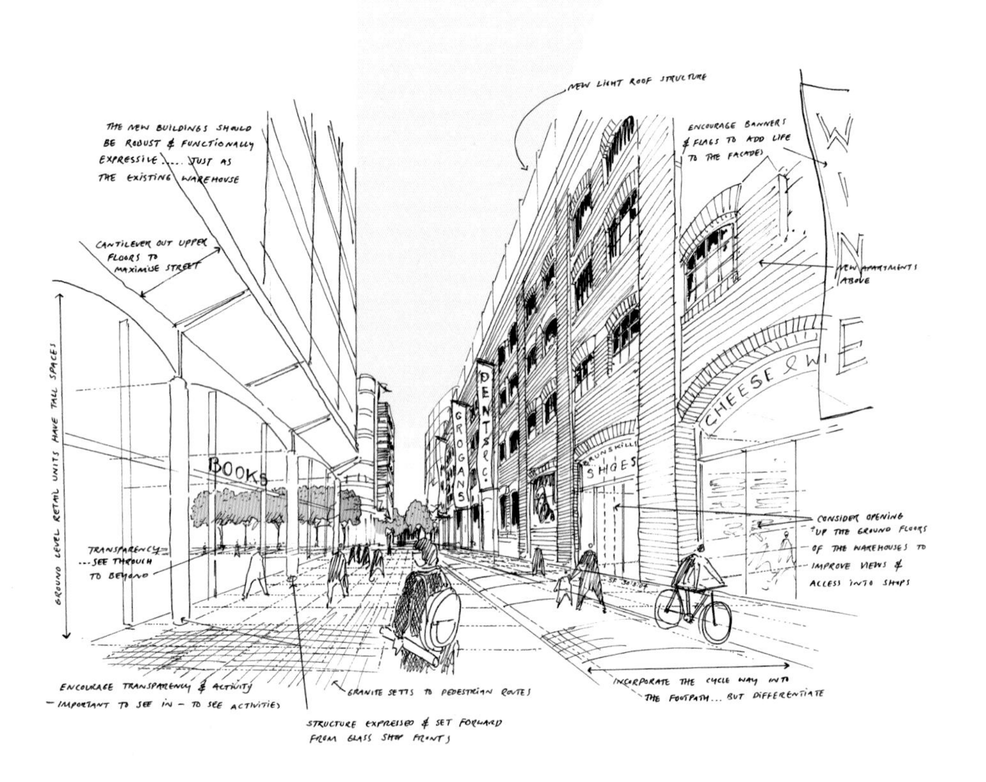

Hopkins Architects was commissioned in 2002 by EastsideCity Developments to prepare masterplanning proposals for three sites on the eastern edge of the city centre, all within the Eastside Regeneration Zone as defined by the city's Local Plan. By far the largest of these sites includes the former 'island', occupied for more than a century by Boots (which largely moved out in the 1990s), and also the former Great Northern Station (closed in 1988, but now restored and occupied by Holmes Place) and the adjacent Great Northern and James Alexander warehouses. The masterplan also looked at the bus garage site to the north and beyond at the site of Sneinton Market, a run-down facility that remains the heart of a busy retail area. The masterplan outlines the aim to create "a new vibrant and mixed-use urban quarter. A place that builds on the historic links to the past, but also sets out a vision for new ways of living in Nottingham." Outline planning consent for the Eastside Regeneration Zone proposals was granted in 2005.

This is an area of the city that has suffered from long-term neglect and generally mediocre new development. The canal link to the Island site was, regrettably, completely infilled in the 1990s, and new developments there lack any overall urban discipline, being isolated objects in a generally bleak setting. The largest of these structures is a complex of off-the-peg distribution sheds. The listed Great Northern warehouse, designed by T.C. Hine, remains utterly derelict and at risk. Other industrial buildings on the site that might have had potential for reuse have been demolished within the last twenty years. Much of the land is simply vacant.

A key aim of the local authority was to secure a genuinely mixed-use development, including commercial, employment-generating space alongside residential accommodation. The ongoing renaissance of the canal corridor (for which Hopkins' Inland Revenue headquarters was a major catalyst) provided a strong impetus for the extension of the regeneration process eastwards, beyond Midland Station. The Hopkins masterplan envisages a renewed Sneinton Market, with new housing and live/work spaces surrounding the stalls, and parking below. The bus garage site will contain housing, retail and leisure uses, including (potentially) a new swimming pool. Both these sites are linked by a new boulevard leading to the heart of the extended Island site, which forms the core of the entire Eastside project.

Although it is close to the city centre – within 500 m (550 yd) walking distance of the Lace Market – the Island site is cut off by busy roads and lacks convenient pedestrian connections. Its integration into the city is a prime objective, with the potential for a new tram link that could eventually extend southwards to the Waterside quarter. Within the site, a new area of green parkland is formed as a central focus, girdled by a reopened loop of canal. New development takes the form of urban blocks placed on a grid of new streets – proper streets, with pavements and traffic and shops at ground level. The heart of the site, around the park and canal loop, is largely residential, with offices concentrated on the northern edge of the site. This is intended to be a 'walkable' place and, though on-street parking is provided (along with a large multi-storey car park), there is a strong emphasis on the needs of pedestrians and cyclists. Three new squares are created around the former Great Northern Station and the adjacent warehouses, which will be restored and converted to new uses. In terms of their scale,

The masterplan for Eastside, which includes the former Boots 'Island' site, proposes the creation of a mixed-use urban quarter, a natural extension of the city centre, and is designed around a grid of streets, squares and other public spaces.

the new buildings generally take their cue from those in historic streets like High Pavement and Smithy Row. The tallest blocks, including a landmark tower, are located to the eastern edge of the site.

Much in the Eastside masterplan (to be developed in phases, with a total of over 280,000 sq m/3,000,000 sq ft of space) is the familiar stuff of regeneration projects over the last twenty years – Norman Foster's unrealized project for the redevelopment of King's Cross goods yard in London, for example, focused on a new central park. If the regular grid of streets and building blocks seems at first somewhat rigid – and even out of tune with Nottingham – the discipline it imposes may be a necessary ingredient in the creation of a workable city quarter that could link up with further development extending to the banks of the Trent. It certainly marks a refreshing change of heart from the visual anarchy that was the result in this area of the city of planning policies of the recent past, which left the development of urban form purely to chance and ignored issues of connectivity and permeability. One hopes the outcome will be a genuine new city district, not a ghetto for the professional classes, and that the quality of the architecture and landscape will make it an exemplar for the future redevelopment of post-industrial Nottingham.

City of Learning

City of Learning

D.H. Lawrence, who had turned his back on Nottingham in favour of the French Riviera, wrote condescendingly of his Alma Mater, Nottingham University College, that it was "derived from shrewd cash-chemistry/by good Sir Jesse Boot" ('Nottingham's New University', in *Pansies*, 1929). Yet the University of Nottingham (as it became in 1948) is now established as one of Britain's most prestigious higher-education institutions. Its Highfields campus, developed from the 1920s onwards, contains a fascinating stylistic mix of buildings, ranging from the classicism of P. Morley Horder, T.C. Howitt and McMorran & Whitby via the 1960s Modernism of Basil Spence (and the successor practice Renton Howard Wood) to the Post-modernism of Graham Brown's Djanogly Arts Centre of the 1990s. The green parkland setting tends to be the predominant image of the campus, but there are outstanding buildings to be discovered. Designed by the practice of Faulkner-Brown, Hendy, Watkinson and Stonor (now Faulkner Browns), the Hallward Library, opened in 1973, is as much a landmark in the history of library design as YRM's earlier building for Sheffield University or the Cambridge History Faculty Library by James Stirling. Rigorously planned, precisely detailed and still retaining the majority of its original furnishings, the building reflects the influence of American campus architecture on British institutions and deserves to be treasured as a classic of its period. (Faulkner Browns returned to Nottingham in the mid-1990s to design the fine new university pool.) Julian Marsh's Lakeside Arts Centre is conceived in a very different spirit, with history and context as drivers, and commemorates the university's connection with Lawrence. The development of Hopkins Architects' Jubilee Campus, marking the new millennium, underlined the university's link with the city and is a major regenerative project, using a redundant industrial site. (Proposals for a

The range of academic and research buildings includes BDP's 2003 Breast Institute at the City Hospital (top), the 1970s Hallward Library at the University of Nottingham (above left and right), and the Jubilee Campus (opposite), begun in 1996.

Howitt's Portland Building at the University of Nottingham has been sensitively extended by Hopkins Architects (left). NTU's Boots Library centres on a day-lit central atrium and is a pioneering exercise in low-energy design (opposite).

major extension of the Jubilee Campus, master-planned by London practice Make Architects, were announced in 2005.) More recently Hopkins Architects was commissioned by the University of Nottingham (following a competition in 2000) to extend the Portland Building on the Highfields campus. T.C. Howitt's coldly classical pile occupies a sloping site above the lake. Its principal façade is faced in Portland stone; to the rear, decent brickwork had to suffice. The Hopkins scheme gave the building a three-storey addition to the rear, extending its use as the main student centre on campus. Shops, a new bar, a travel agency and other facilities are included. The extension is faced in reconstituted stone (also used extensively by Hopkins at the Inland Revenue headquarters and produced locally by Trent Concrete) with a glazed atrium connecting it to the Portland Building.

Attached, both physically and academically, to the university, the Queen's Medical Centre incorporates the 1975 medical school by Building Design Partnership (BDP), a building where functional requirements, rather than any sense of delight, prevail. The footbridge connecting the medical school to the main campus is, as Fawcett and Jackson comment in their history of the university's architecture, "unremarkable and rather lumpen". BDP was also responsible for the Breast Institute at Nottingham City Hospital, completed in 2003, where the intelligent use of materials and an open plan create a building that is unthreatening and far removed from the mechanistic aesthetic that infused hospital design for too long.

Nottingham's second university, Nottingham Trent (NTU, formerly Trent Polytechnic), also has a growing international reputation. NTU is based in the city centre, with an architecturally striking core formed by the Gothic Revival Arkwright Building (1877–81, by Lockwood & Mawson) and T.C. Howitt's extraordinary Newton Building of the 1950s. The constraints of the university's central location are reflected in the design of the Boots Library, a new city landmark at the junction of Shakespeare Street and Goldsmith Street, designed by James McArtney Architects (exterior) and ECD (interior). The exterior is

A former art college, now NTU's Waverley Building, was sympathetically refurbished and extended in 1999–2000 to house art, design and architecture departments (opposite and above). High Pavement College occupies a new building on Chaucer Street (right). Completed in 2002, it is a dramatic symbol of the city's educational renaissance.

marred by skimped details. The interior, however, really sings, responding to changing ideas about the nature and purpose of libraries, with a central atrium bringing natural light to the heart of the building. Inside, ECD worked to a client brief demanding a high degree of energy efficiency and the use of sustainable materials.

Though very much a new-generation university, NTU has inherited an attractive portfolio of vintage buildings, which it is seeking to upgrade for present-day needs. East Midlands-based practice Evans Vettori was responsible for the restoration, refurbishment and extension (1999–2000) of the listed 1860s Waverley Building, housing the university's art, design and architecture departments. The building had been considerably extended in the 1950s, with a large teaching block north of the main building that had to be retained. By demolishing an unattractive infill at the rear, however, Evans Vettori gave the complex a new social heart, linking the original Victorian art school and the 1950s extension. The addition addresses, in fact, a number of practical requirements, including that for full disabled access, and is elegantly and minimally detailed to a quality that belies the modest budget for the project. Ugly partitioning was removed from the ground floor of the 1860s building to create a light-filled exhibition space that is open to the public. On the top floor, more partitions have been stripped out to create a magnificent, flexible studio space beneath the great roof beams. All in all, the project exemplifies the movement in Nottingham to capitalize on the heritage of the past and make it work for today. Hopkins Architects' project to redevelop the area between the Arkwright and Newton buildings (see pp.122–23) has similar aspirations, giving NTU a real heart, though the degree of demolition proposed has proved contentious.

Further evidence of the ongoing revolution in educational provision is provided by new city schools. High Pavement Sixth Form College 'came home' to the city centre in 2002 – it was founded as the Unitarian Day Charity School on High Pavement in the Lace Market in 1788, and moved out firstly to Forest Fields in the 1890s and then to Bestwood in the 1950s, where it became a sixth-form college. Now part of New College Nottingham (also responsible for the refurbishment of Hine's Adams Building, see pp. 48–51), the college occupies a £6.3 million centre, catering for 1000 students, on Chaucer Street, designed by Ellis Williams Architects on a design-and-build contract. Foster and Partners' Djanogly City Academy, opened in 2005, is another example of innovative design responding to innovative educational ideas. The academy, sponsored by Sir Harry Djanogly, specializes in information technology, and the building, arranged around a naturally lit internal street, provides highly flexible teaching areas around communal spaces that encourage interaction and social contact. An asset for use by the local community as well as its students, the academy epitomizes the role of education in the regeneration of Nottingham.

Swimming Pool University of Nottingham

Faulkner Browns 1995–96

Faulkner Browns, the practice that had given the University of Nottingham its outstanding new library in the 1970s, was an astute choice for the university's new pool, commissioned twenty years later. The result is a building of simple, understated elegance that will probably age more gracefully than some of the excursions into styling that have strayed on to the campus in recent decades, further confusing its architectural image.

The university had made use of P. Morley Horder's lakeside lido until it was demolished in the 1980s to make room for the new Djanogly Arts Centre. It was subsequently decided to locate a new covered pool at the north-east corner of the campus, close to the utilitarian 1970s sports hall. The new pool was opened in 1996 and cost £2.25 million. In the tradition of the glasshouses of the nineteenth century, the building makes a virtue of its essentially functional agenda. The 25 m x 18 m (82 x 59 ft) pool is intended to meet the needs of both competition swimmers and those for whom swimming is simply healthy recreation. Also included within the building envelope are the usual changing and other facilities. The internal space is covered by a series of eight pin-jointed steel portal frames that are extended along the sides of the building to form a sunshading external grille. The exposed steel frame is infilled with green-tinted glass, translucent in effect and very much in tune with the sylvan setting. The roof vault is filled with polycarbonate glazing.

The architects wanted to create a 'pavilion in the park'; they have achieved their aim admirably with this simple and elegant project.

The over-sailing roof of the University Pool provides external sunshading and internally sweeps up to provide swimmers with a dramatic space.

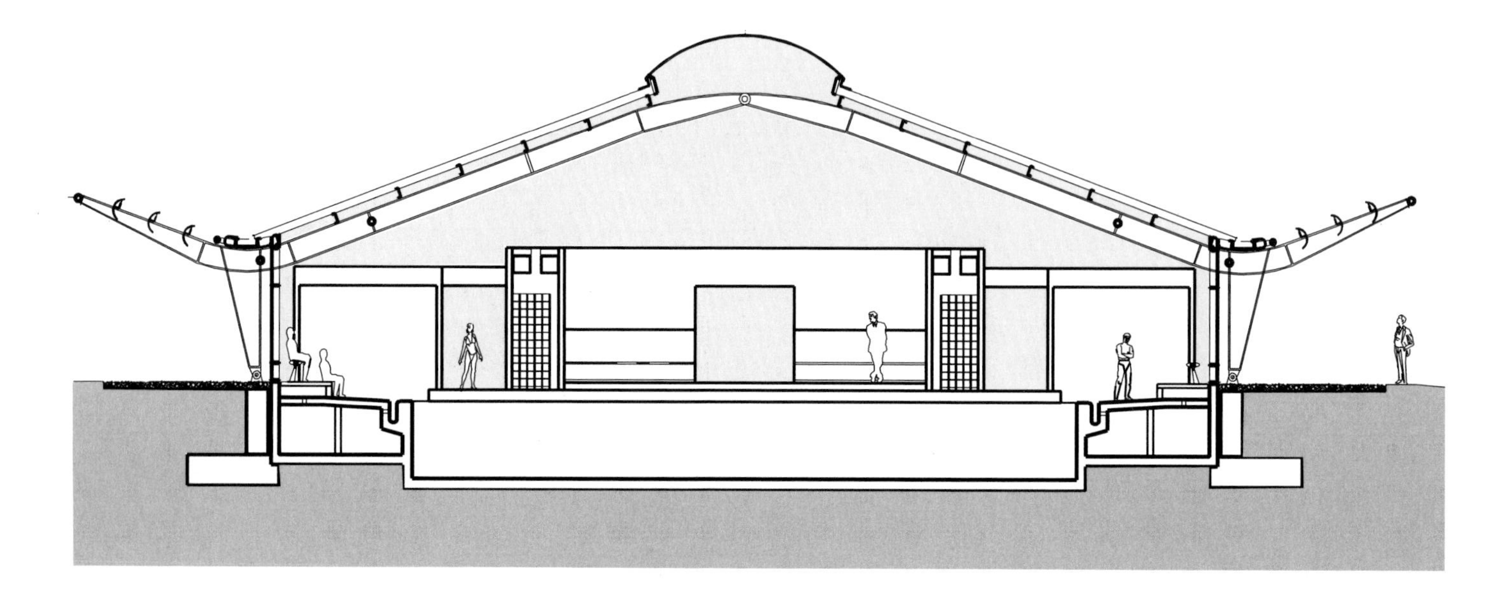

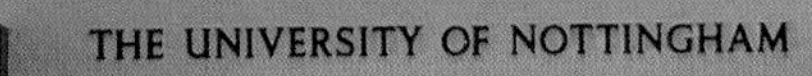
SPEEDO
THE UNIVERSITY OF NOTTINGHAM

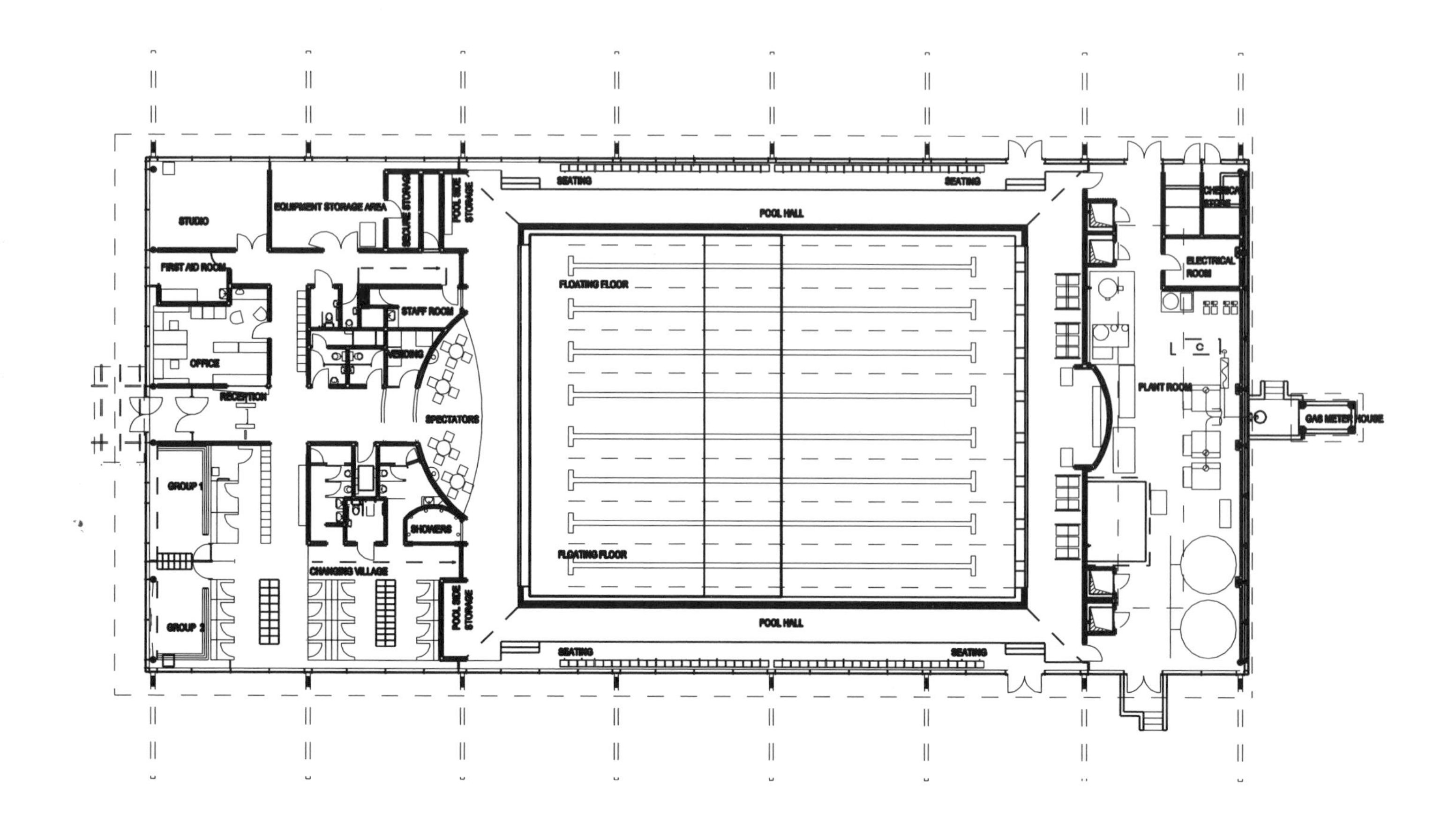
STUDIO
EQUIPMENT STORAGE AREA
SECURE STORAGE
POOL SIDE STORAGE
FIRST AID ROOM
STAFF ROOM
OFFICE
VENDING
RECEPTION
SPECTATORS
GROUP 1
SHOWERS
CHANGING VILLAGE
GROUP 2
POOL SIDE STORAGE
SEATING
SEATING
POOL HALL
FLOATING FLOOR
FLOATING FLOOR
POOL HALL
SEATING
SEATING
ELECTRICAL ROOM
PLANT ROOM

Designed on a rational plan, structurally simple and elegantly detailed, the pool, with its memories of the glasshouse architecture of the nineteenth century, is an appropriate addition to the parkland campus of the University of Nottingham.

CASE STUDY

Jubilee Campus University of Nottingham

Hopkins Architects 1996–2004

Michael Hopkins's relationship with the University of Nottingham extends back to the 1960s when, as a young assistant, he worked for Basil Spence on the new science blocks at the Highfields campus. More relevant to the success of Michael Hopkins & Partners (as it then was) in the 1996 competition for the university's new campus was the fact that it had recently completed the Inland Revenue headquarters just down the road, a sensational addition to the city's fabric that attracted widespread critical acclaim.

The University's Jubilee Campus (where development is still continuing; see pp. 120–21) is, in many respects, a pivotal development for the university. In the 1920s, thanks to the munificence of Jesse Boot, the university left the city centre for the green sward of Highfields and developed a classic suburban campus there in a frankly American mould. The Jubilee Campus marks the university's re-engagement with the city. Relieving the pressure for over-intensive development at Highfields, which is a surprisingly short distance away, it makes excellent use of a 'brownfield' ex-industrial site, addressing the ongoing rise in student numbers and equipping Nottingham (a university in the Russell Group, a self-selected group of large research-led universities) to compete for talent and funding in a global higher-education market. The Jubilee Campus (the project marked the fiftieth anniversary of the university's Royal Charter) provides the University of Nottingham with an alternative image, more streetwise and up-to-the-minute than that of white classical façades and green lawns.

The site was formerly occupied by the low-rise sheds of the Raleigh Cycle factory and associated Sturmey Archer gearbox factory at the interface of an area of industry with one of inter-war suburban housing. The intention was to include residential accommodation as well as teaching facilities for three faculties. The Jubilee Campus's urban density notwithstanding, there are parallels with Highfields, most obviously in the integration of architecture and landscape. Hopkins's key move was to create an irregular linear lake along the western edge of the site, reinforcing an existing tree belt screening nearby housing. The teaching blocks – a central facility known as the Exchange, with three large lecture theatres, and blocks accommodating computer science, education, continuing education and the business school – are ranged along the waterside, with residential buildings set behind. (A postgraduate residential complex is located at the northern end of the site, close to the lake.) Covered colonnades, evoking those of nineteenth-century docklands warehouses, provide sheltered spots to linger en route from one building to another. The circular library (or 'learning resource centre') is dramatically set in the water.

During the 1990s, Hopkins's architecture seemed to turn away from its 'high-tech' roots towards a preoccupation with place and history. In some respects, the Jubilee Campus appears to be a return to those roots in its economy, rationality and use of repetitive components and forms. The aesthetic is one of exposed in-situ concrete, galvanized steel and prefabricated panels of low-cost cedar cladding (now weathered to a mellow grey hue). The faculty buildings share a repetitive plan – three-storey blocks of offices and teaching space linked by

The Exchange building at the heart of the campus contains three large lecture theatres dramatically stacked to form a prominent feature of the central atrium (above; opposite bottom). The circular library has become iconic, a symbol of the campus's transformation of the surrounding area (opposite top).

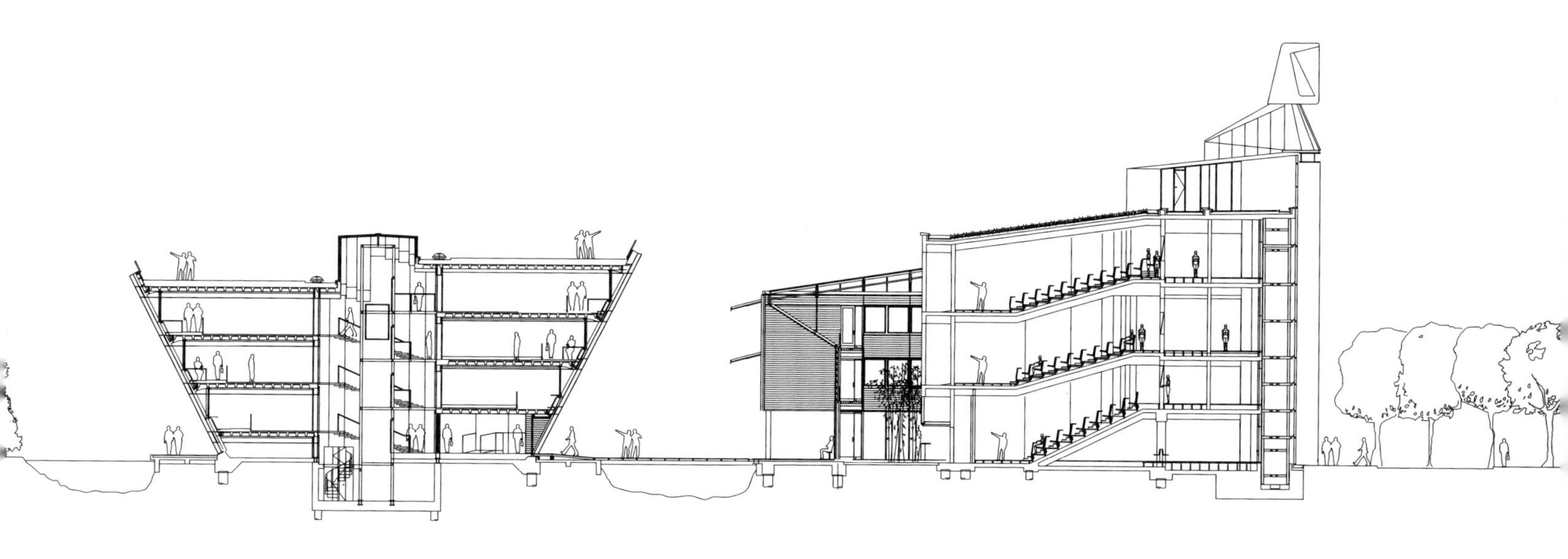

The campus has formed a new academic quarter a mile from the main campus on a site which was formerly industrial desert. Popular with students, the new environment includes meeting-places and promenades and is intended as a launchpad for the masterplan of the surrounding area.

full-height glazed atria. A double-width atrium between the schools of computer science and education houses a large refectory. The library (criticized by Peter Fawcett for its "wilful frivolity") is a delight, its internal spiral ramp so obviously inspired by Frank Lloyd Wright's Solomon R. Guggenheim Museum in New York, and its playful form offsetting the cool rationalism of the other buildings.

The form and structural content of the buildings, as well as the surrounding landscape, are ingredients in a sophisticated low-energy services strategy that takes advantage of passive solar and wind energy to heat, cool and ventilate the internal spaces. The distinctive rooftop cowls, as much symbolic as functional, are used to exhaust stale air and incorporate heat recovery systems for use in winter. Sunshades, external louvres, good insulation, opening windows, photovoltaic cells and planted roofs, however, all contribute to a significant reduction in CO2 emissions of more than 2500 tonnes (2460 tons) annually compared to conventional buildings of comparable size. Perhaps the most obviously energy-saving aspect of the scheme is its virtuoso use of controlled daylight to provide benign working conditions on all but the most dismal day. The role of the Jubilee Campus as a pioneering exercise in environmentally friendly design is not the least important aspect of the project, and it has won international recognition.

The first phase of the campus was completed in 1999. The new business school at the south end of the site was opened in 2004 – sadly, though formally a Hopkins building, the quality of detail found in the earlier buildings on the

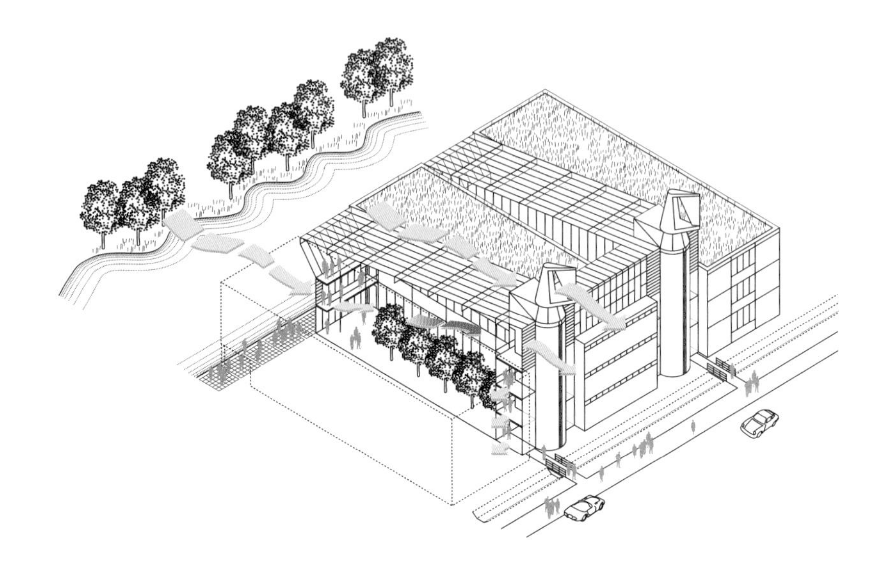

site seems to have been sacrificed to the exigencies of a design-and-build contract. At the southern end of the lake, the Hopkins-designed 9000 sq m (96,900 sq ft) National College for School Leadership, completed in 2002, is a residential centre for school leaders, its aesthetic and low-energy agenda in line with the model established by the Jubilee Campus.

The further development of the campus is to proceed in line with a masterplan drawn up by Make Architects, which is currently working on its first building for the site.

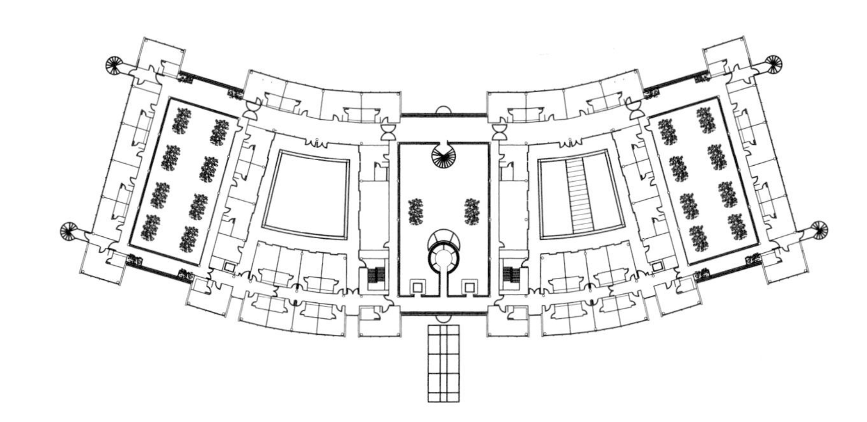

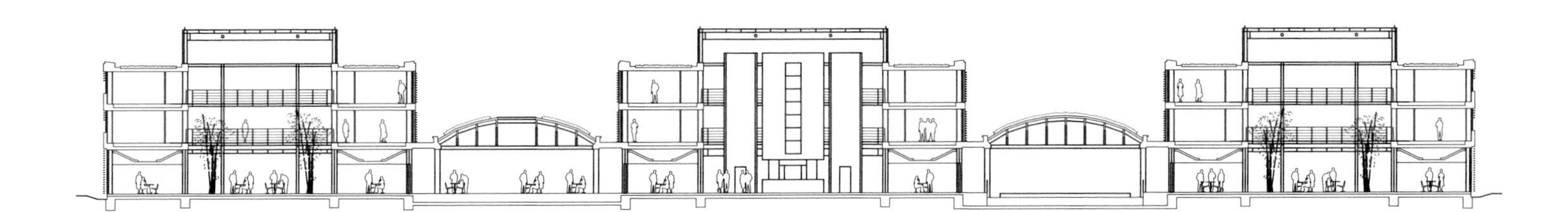

CASE STUDY

Djanogly City Academy Gregory Boulevard

Foster and Partners 2002–05

Characteristic of the Foster office in its elegant minimalism, the Djanogly City Academy adapts the vocabulary of modern workplace design to the field of education.

City academies are now an established, though still controversial, component of the educational scene. Nottingham's first city academy, sponsored by Sir Harry Djanogly and specializing in information and communications technology, was founded in 2003, replacing the heavily oversubscribed Djanogly City Technology College; the latter's premises on Sherwood Rise now house the academy's centre for fourteen- to nineteen-year-olds. Foster and Partners' building, on the site of the demolished Forest Comprehensive School in Gregory Boulevard, is part of a radical attempt to elevate standards in a very disadvantaged neighbourhood, and caters for more than eight hundred eleven- to fourteen-year-olds. It is classic Foster: cool and minimal, with transparency and legibility as the key drivers of the design.

The site of the former comprehensive school was set on a natural rise further back from the road; the siting of the new building opens up land to the rear, appropriately levelled, for sports and recreation use. The plan is linear, with all teaching, social and ancillary spaces arranged along a double-height, top-lit internal street, criss-crossed by bridge links at first-floor level. Classroom and specialist teaching areas are provided on two levels, with double-height spaces at either end of the building housing art, dance and theatre studios, a sports hall, a restaurant and the entrance hall with its library and a cybercafé. (The stress on new information technology means that every student is equipped with a notebook computer, used for 80% of classes. The radical working environment is wireless and almost entirely paperless.) By locating all communal and social spaces at the eastern end of the building, their use, out of school hours, by the local community is facilitated; teaching zones are then closed off.

Flexibility has long been a Foster preoccupation, and the use of non-load-bearing partitions within the steel-framed structure provides scope for the interior to be extensively reconfigured in line with an ever-changing learning agenda. On the first floor, the 'home bases' provided for the three year-groups into which students are divided feature moveable partitions to allow for varying class sizes.

The building is designed for economical, low-energy running. Natural ventilation is provided via high-level vents on the northern elevation, and opening roof lights. Opening the vents at night allows the exposed concrete floors to be used as a thermal 'sink', providing natural cooling by day. The southern façade to Gregory Boulevard is sealed and fitted with extensive shading, with mechanical ventilation to the spaces behind. Chilled beams provide an economical way of cooling the classrooms on the upper level, where the students' computers generate a lot of heat.

It is the businesslike and straightforward nature of this building that impresses: there is no rhetoric, no reference to the traditional educational vernacular. The aim of the institution is to equip young people to pursue successful careers in business, so that the aesthetic, that of a corporate headquarters, is entirely in tune with that agenda.

Djanogly
City Academy Nottingham

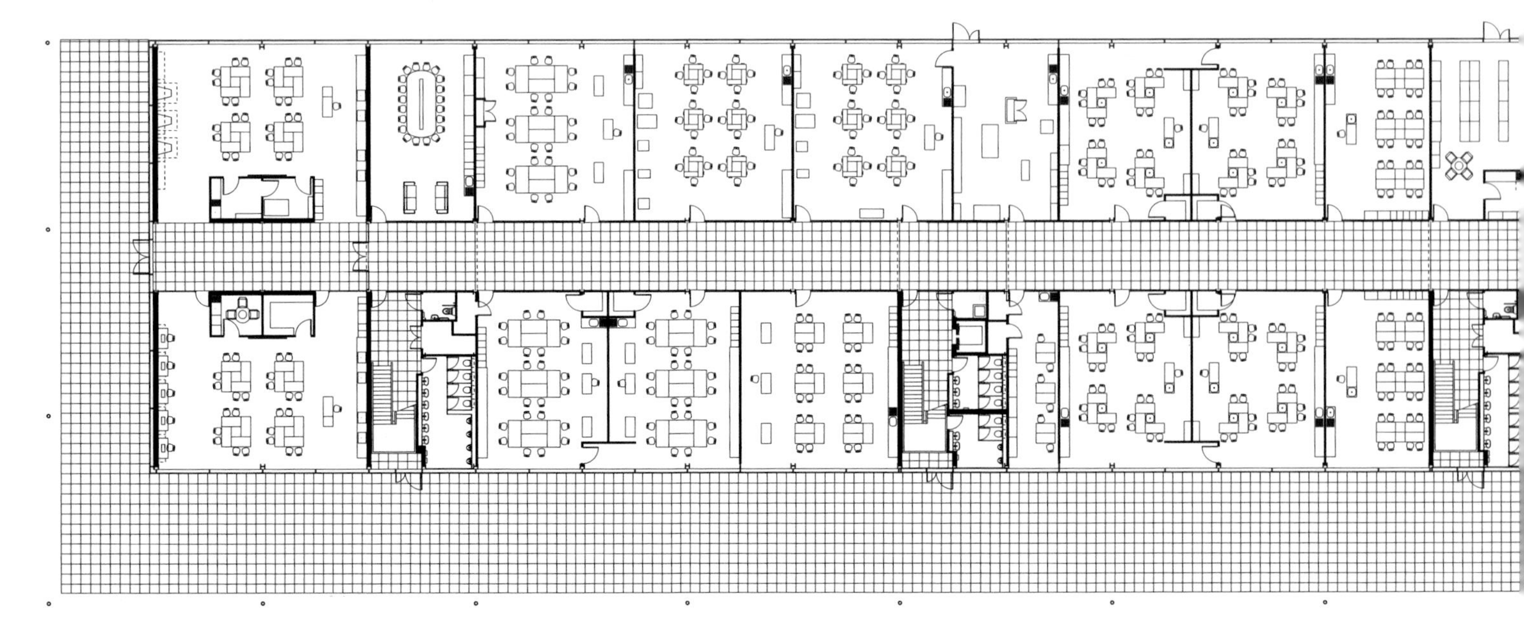

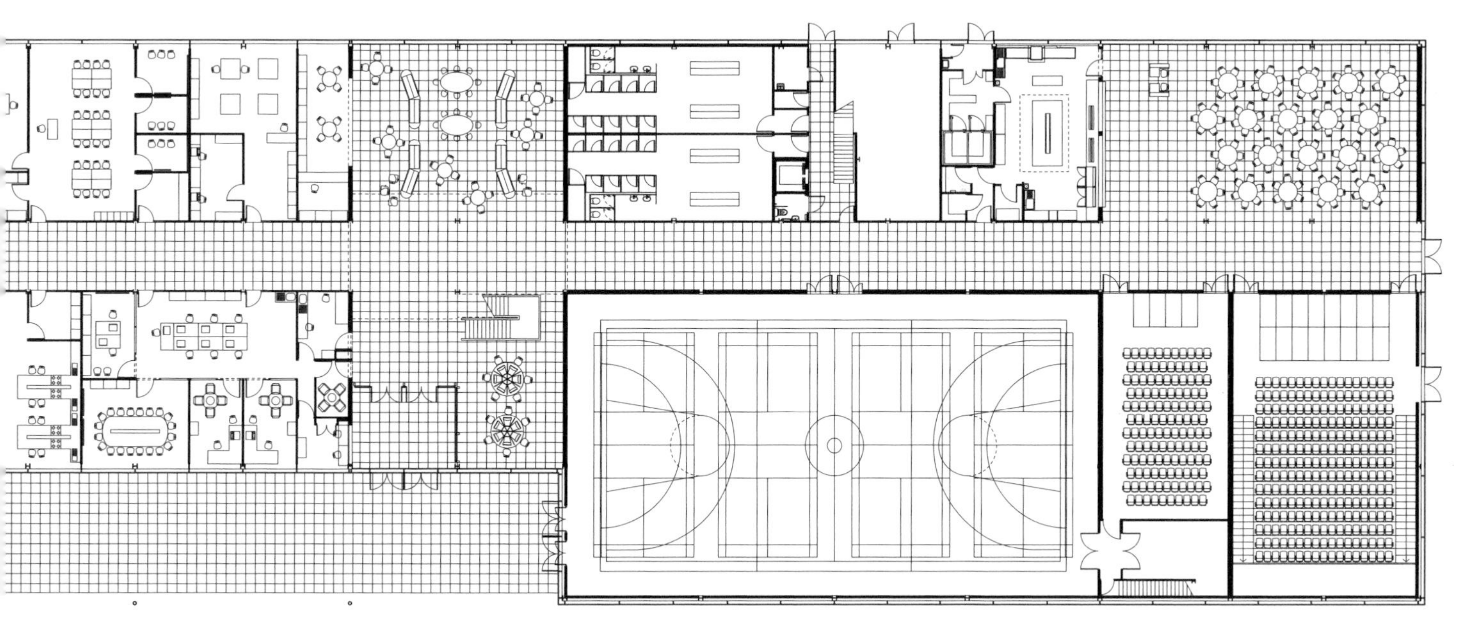

The naturally lit internal street is the operational heart of the building (opposite). The reception area extends into the open-plan library and study area (top). The highly rational plan (above): ground-floor level includes the sports hall, lecture theatres and an open-plan café.

Jubilee Campus University of Nottingham Phase 2

Make Architects 2006–08

The University of Nottingham's expansion continues, both at home – it has more than 25,000 students in Nottingham – and abroad (since 2000 Nottingham has had a campus in Malaysia, and in 2005 opened one in Ningbo, China, complete with an extraordinary copy of P. Morley Horder's Trent Building). The university's expansion during the 1990s focused on the development of the new Jubilee Campus (see pp. 112–15), the work of Michael Hopkins and a remarkably successful fusion of architecture and landscape on a former factory site. In 2005 the university resolved not to proceed with Hopkins' proposals for a further phase of the Jubilee Campus, but to commission instead Make Architects, the practice founded in 2004 by Ken Shuttleworth, formerly a director of Foster and Partners.

Despite the success of the Hopkins campus, the Make masterplan abandons the mix of an orthogonal building grid with lavish planting for a more dynamic approach that appears to stem from Shuttleworth's extensive experience in the field of commercial development. The formally linear quality of the proposed landscape recalls that at More London (1998–), the Thames-side development in which Shuttleworth was heavily involved in his days with Foster and Partners. The gateway 'volcano' building promises to have the eye-catching qualities of some recent City of London office schemes and will form part of the first 7 ha (18 acre), £29 million phase of the new development, along with International House, essentially an administration block, flanked by a new teaching building – the aim is to complete these three buildings by the end of 2007. The aesthetic of the new buildings ditches Hopkins's timber-clad façades in favour of layered, colourful frontages in which extensive use is made of terracotta. There are plans for a sculptural landmark tower which Shuttleworth hopes will have some of the impact of the Skylon, a key feature of the 1951 Festival of Britain. The detailed design of the buildings will incorporate a progressive low-energy heating and ventilation programme: the university is anxious to be seen as an advocate of sustainable development.

The longer-term development of the masterplan, which could certainly include a new science and research park, depends on the university's acquisition of additional industrial land in the Triumph Road area. A City Council development brief published in 2004 earmarked all this land for university use.

Make Architects' extension to the Jubilee Campus reflects an approach radically different from that of Hopkins Architects, and includes new buildings for administration, teaching and business (above), all designed to an aesthetic of strong form and vivid colour.

Nottingham Trent University

Hopkins Architects
2007–09

Hopkins Architects' project for NTU's city-centre campus fuses the nineteenth-century Arkwright Building (opposite top) and the 1950s Newton Building (right), creating a new quadrangle between the two and rationalizing the present maze of spaces (opposite bottom).

Nottingham Trent University (NTU) is one of the largest and most successful of the 'new' universities, with some 27,000 students. It has inherited in its main city-centre campus the original Nottingham University College Arkwright Building and the landmark 1950s former technical college Newton Building. When Howitt built Newton, he conceived it as the first stage of a larger scheme, including the demolition and redevelopment of Arkwright. The two buildings, though adjacent, therefore do not relate to each other at all. Both listed buildings are now in need of major renovation and investment, and no longer meet the needs of a twenty-first-century university. The engineering labs of Howitt's technical college are no longer used. Engineering teaching is now done on computers.

NTU has commissioned Hopkins Architects to re-order these two buildings as part of a new core central teaching and student facility for the university. Ingeniously, Hopkins Architects have been able to come up with a plan that makes sense of the complex internal arrangements of the two buildings (Arkwright in particular is a warren of disconnected elements) and relates the two buildings in a coherent whole. The key to the plan is a splendid new entrance atrium from Goldsmith Street which, with its new tram stop, is now the campus's focal point. This replaces a dreary 1960s building and a service yard.

The fine street elevations of the buildings are entirely retained. A critical but positive intervention would be the demolition of parts of the central wing of the Arkwright building to create a practical layout allowing the buildings to be used effectively, and to create a new 'quadrangle', a new publicly accessible external space the campus currently lacks. The scheme is a massive investment in the renovation of the two most important civic buildings of their respective eras, and will secure their long-term future as the heart of the university, one of the most dynamic elements of the city's future.

City of Culture

City of Culture

Victorian Nottingham failed to acquire some of the trappings of cultural achievement that graced other large cities – a grand concert hall, for example, or a purpose-built city art gallery to compare with those in Manchester, Liverpool or Birmingham – although theatres and music halls thrived. Most of these have long vanished, and most of the city's historic cinemas have gone the same way. Those that survive, the Elite, for instance, or the Metropole in Sherwood, no longer serve their original purpose. Nonetheless the city fathers of the Victorian period showed foresight in acquiring the ruins of the castle, converted by T.C. Hine into a public art museum of unique character. (A recent refurbishment by Derek Latham has provided facilities in line with modern visitor expectations.) Wollaton Hall, an extraordinary Elizabethan mansion, was bought by the city in 1924, minus contents, and later became a museum of natural history, a use highly popular with generations of local children though not necessarily in tune with its setting.

The construction of the Playhouse in the 1960s put the city ahead in the cultural investment stakes and the building has worn well, benefiting from a recent extension and refurbishment project by Marsh Grochowski Architects. The city further demonstrated its commitment to the arts with the acquisition from the Moss Empire chain of the 1860s Theatre Royal (designed by C.J. Phipps, with a splendid later auditorium by Frank Matcham) and its refurbishment in the 1970s. The project was the first of a series of major theatre refurbishments carried out by the practice of Renton Howard Wood Levin (RHWL) under Nicholas Thompson, with Clare Ferraby responsible for the restoration of the historic interiors. At a cost (which now

Converted into an art gallery in the nineteenth century, Nottingham Castle has recently been refurbished to provide modern visitor facilities (this page). Marsh Grochowski's D.H. Lawrence Pavilion on the University of Nottingham campus (opposite) enlivens the public park created in the 1920s.

The County Hotel, shown opposite in 1927, was controversially demolished to make way for the Royal Complex, of which the Theatre Royal (above) is part.

seems modest) of £3.3 million, it gave the city a prestigious 1000-seat venue for everything from variety shows and musicals to ballet and opera.

One price that had to be paid for saving the Theatre Royal was the demolition of the County (formerly Clarendon) Hotel that stood immediately to the west on the site earmarked for new backstage spaces, including dressing rooms and scenery dock. Facilities for both audience and performers were so poor before the reconstruction that the theatre faced closure. Backstage facilities were rudimentary and many companies declined to perform in the theatre. A second failing of the old theatre was the relative paucity of foyer and bar spaces and the poor vertical circulation. New foyer areas, including an impressive staircase, cloakrooms and bars, were constructed east of the existing theatre. The additions eschew pastiche and are designed to defer externally to Phipps's fine portico. Internally, they have a faintly Deco quality not inappropriate in a theatre. The auditorium was restored by Clare Ferraby using colours of a late Victorian 'Aesthetic' character, and was the subject of a comprehensive technical upgrade.

The Royal Concert Hall project (the subject of fierce political controversy at the time) followed on from the refurbishment of the Theatre Royal, and the two were conceived by RHWL in tandem. The 2500-seat Concert Hall opened in 1983. It occupies a site behind the Theatre Royal, and its externally glazed foyers (using the reflective glass fashionable at the time) are intended to contrast with the more solid exteriors of the extensions to the theatre. The main entrance is marked by a colonnade which echoes that of the Theatre Royal. The Royal Centre, the collective name for the theatre and concert hall, was a vital move that underpinned the dynamism of the city centre before the present wave of private-sector investment in leisure had materialized.

Creative industries are now seen as prime movers in urban regeneration. The Broadway

The Royal Concert Hall was opened in 1983 on a site behind the 1865 Theatre Royal, to which its glazed exterior presents a dramatic contrast. The Royal Centre is an important cultural venue for the city of Nottingham.

Broadway (right), a media centre launched in 1980 and including an arts cinema, is to be extended with new foyer spaces in a glazed extension to Broad Street (below right).

Cinema, opened in the 1960s as an independent film theatre, now forms part of the Nottingham Media Centre on Broad Street, close to the Lace Market. Broadway is, in fact, a much-altered Methodist chapel, bizarrely reclad in 1950s terrazzo. The centre, launched in the 1980s, now includes production suites, a café-bar and a smaller 150-seat screen opened in 1992. In the second, £1.5 million phase of work by architects Burrell Foley Fischer (appointed in 1990), the main cinema block was linked to an adjacent administration building by a new glazed infill (4 m/13 ft wide) containing stairs and lifts (with full disabled access), and the main auditorium refurbished with a new gallery above the foyer. There are ongoing plans to remodel the Broad Street frontage with foyer spaces on three levels behind a glazed façade pushed forward of the existing colonnaded elevation.

While established art forms are now well provided for in Nottingham, the city's arts provision is expanding to address new needs. Promotion of contemporary visual art in the city has long been left to private galleries, such as the Angel Row Gallery, but the proposed Centre for Contemporary Art Nottingham (CCAN), designed by Caruso St John (see pp. 54–55), will give the city a facility of international quality showcasing both 'object' and performance art. Hawkins Brown's New Art Exchange at Hyson Green is specifically designed to promote forms of artistic expression associated with minority groups.

Taking into account the dynamism of the popular music and jazz scenes in the city, which have received a stimulus from the explosion of Nottingham's nightlife, and the huge input from the city's schools, two universities and colleges, Nottingham can be reckoned a place of intense and varied cultural activity, generating investment in old buildings and the continuing commissioning of innovative new architecture.

CASE STUDY

Playhouse Extension and Sky Mirror

Marsh Grochowski Architects/Anish Kapoor 1994–2001

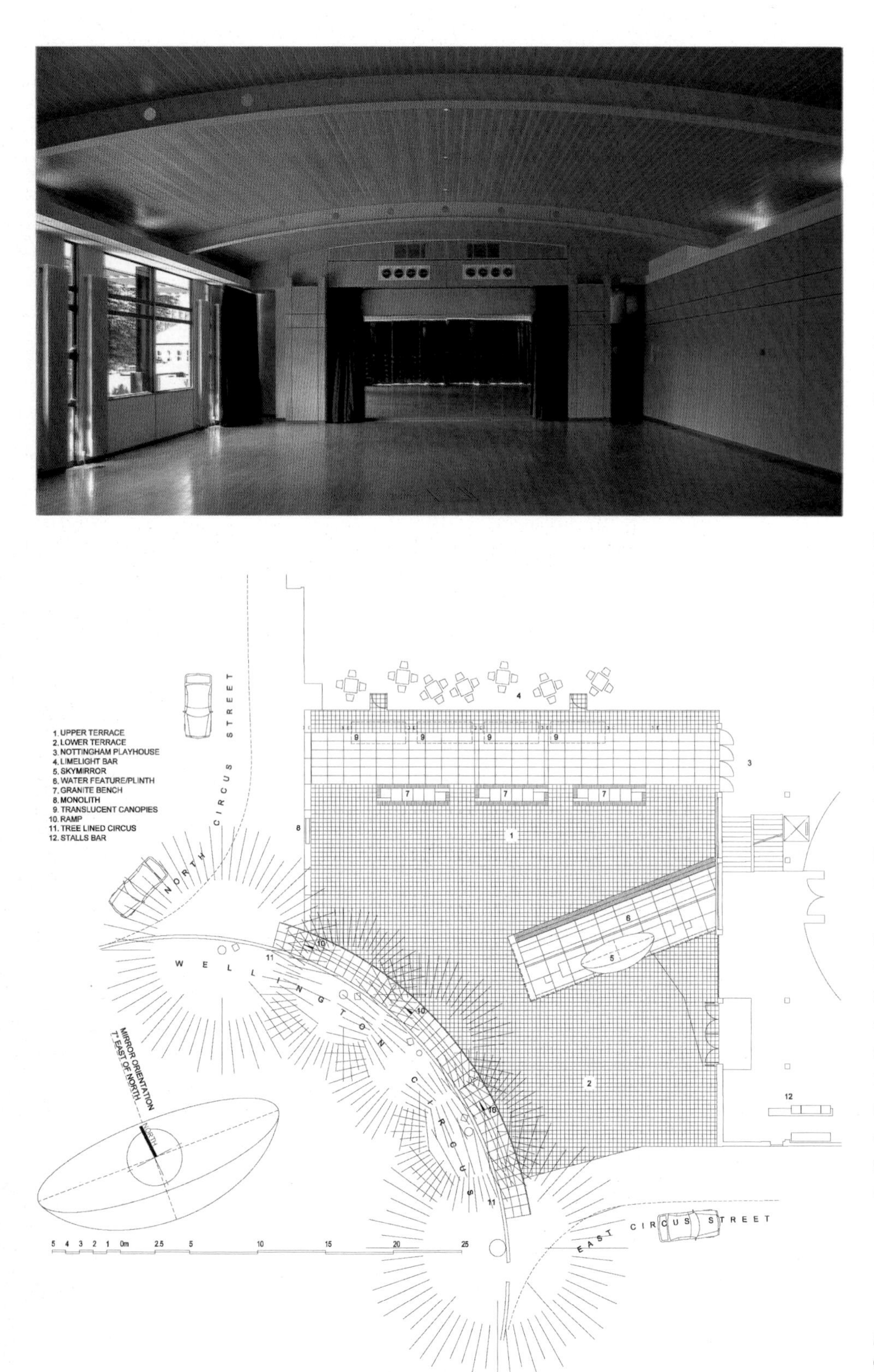

Peter Moro's Playhouse, opened in 1963, has long been recognized as one of the outstanding arts buildings of its period, an enlightened piece of patronage by the local authority that has served Nottingham well over more than forty years. Even a building of this quality, however, must adapt to changing practical needs, which have been addressed by Marsh Grochowski Architects' extension. Far more significant, however, in terms of public perception and amenity, is the new Playhouse Square with its majestic Sky Mirror (2001), a major work by the leading sculptor Anish Kapoor.

Plans to construct an extension to the building led to its listing (at Grade II*) in 1994, though the listing was issued after the new 'Playroom' rehearsal space was subsequently built (with the approval of English Heritage, following some amendments to the original proposals). A roof terrace had been created above the single-storey Limelight Bar in the 1980s, and became the site for the new rehearsal space that the Playhouse so badly needed. The additions are designed in sympathy with Moro's architecture, and have had the beneficial effect of masking the utilitarian flank of the adjacent Albert Hall, left awkwardly exposed by the 1960s development. In conjunction with the projects, the same architects also carried out a refurbishment of the bar and foyer areas.

For many years, the Playhouse had no associated external space. For a decade or so, the area of Wellington Circus in front of it was simply used for car parking. In the 1970s, part of this area was closed off and paved in cobbles as an overspill area for the Limelight Bar. Neither the choice of materials nor the form of the space proved satisfactory, and the paved area, which made little impact against the strong form of the Circus, seemed hardly related to the theatre.

Marsh Grochowski's extension to the Playhouse includes the creation of a first-floor rehearsal space (above left) and the construction of a generous public square where a striking feature is provided by Anish Kapoor's Sky Mirror (opposite).

Elevations showing the new extension and the theatre with its fly tower. The new square (opposite) is designed to integrate the theatre with the life of the city and has proved a highly popular space.

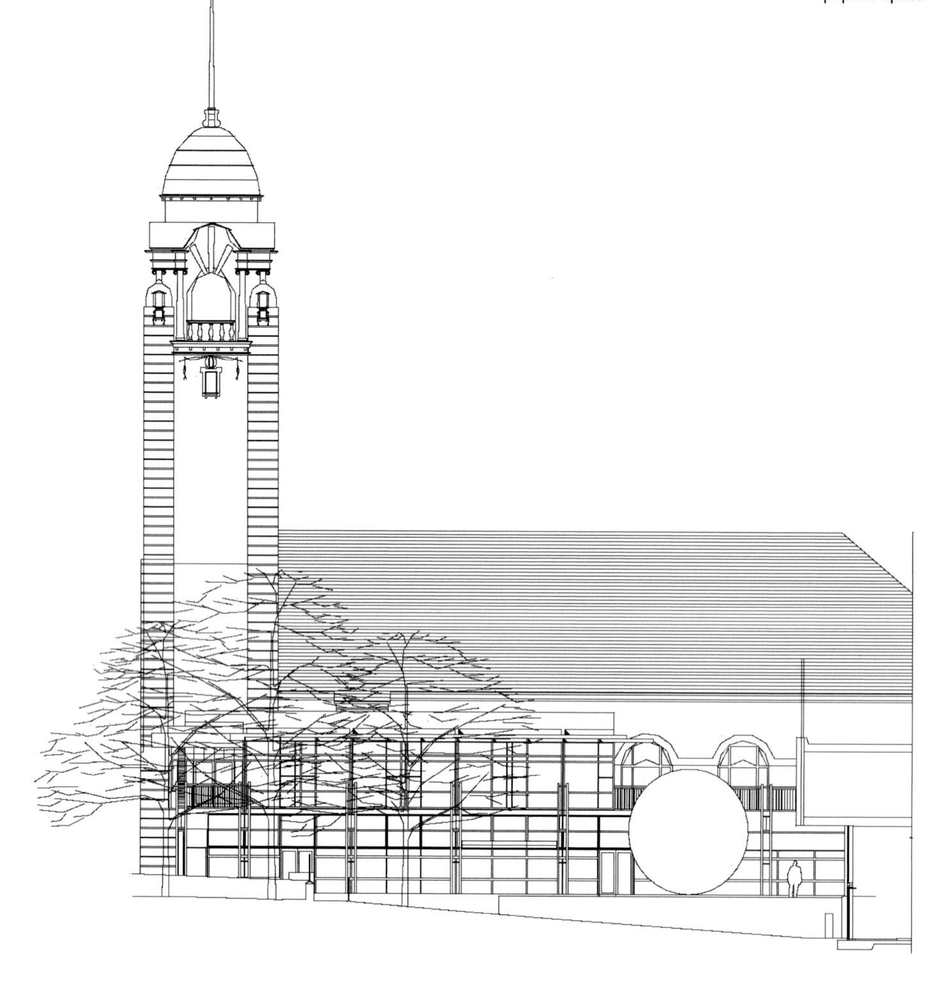

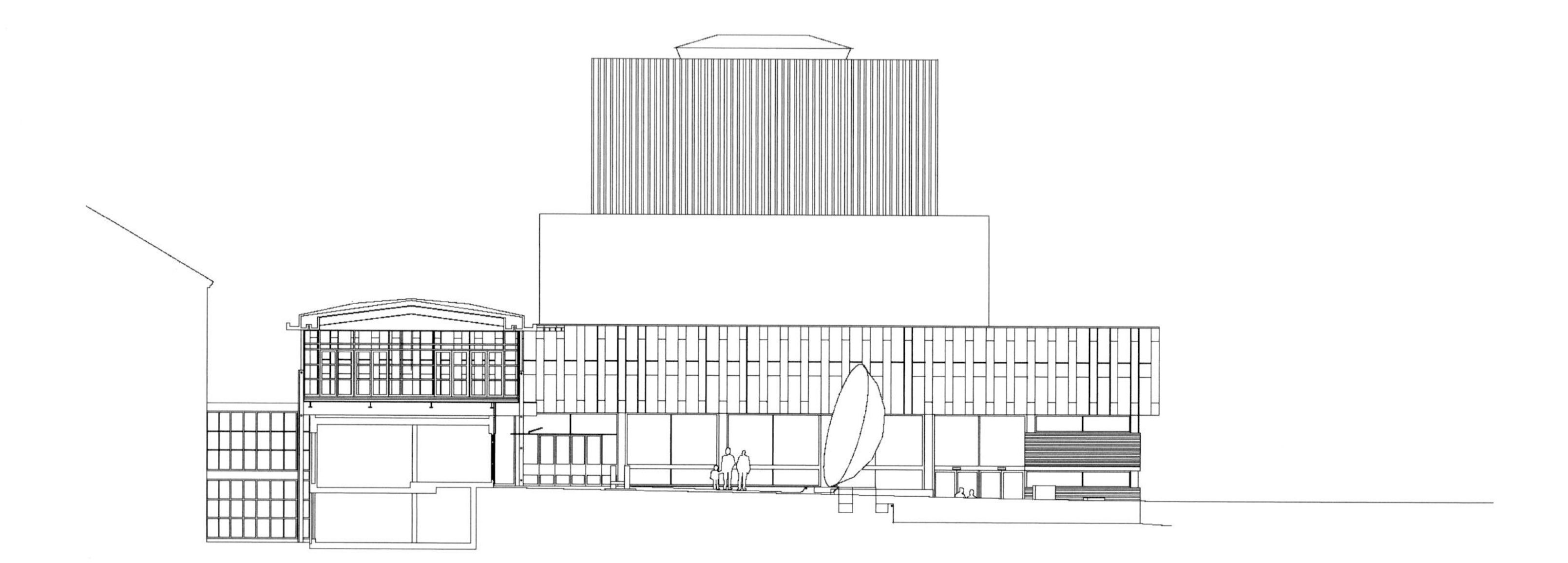

The new Playhouse Square, opened in 2001, was designed by Marsh Grochowksi Architects in association with Anish Kapoor, whose Sky Mirror was an integral element in the £1.2 million scheme. Funded by the Arts Council, with support from the European Regional Development Fund, Sir Harry Djanogly, the Henry Moore Foundation and Nottingham City Council, the 5.75 m (19 ft) diameter concave mirror of polished stainless steel is one of the most riveting works of 'public art' yet achieved in Britain, totally eschewing the triviality and sentimentality associated with some expressions of that genre. The mirror was conceived by Kapoor as a work that makes reference to its context, both physical and human. Its convex side reflects the towers of the Albert Hall and the A.W.N. Pugin Cathedral of St Barnabas – upside down. On the reverse, its effect is that of a funfair mirror, distorting the reflections of theatre-goers who peer into it. The mirror is set on a plinth that sits in a pool of water, providing further, vertical reflections. The mirror had to be carefully positioned, avoiding the danger of reflected sunlight causing uncomfortable and even damaging reflections.

The square is paved with black granite, avoiding steps (despite the fall in the site) and with careful attention to the needs of the disabled. It divides into two distinct areas, with the Sky Mirror on its plinth forming the pivot. The lower courtyard relates naturally to the theatre foyer (with an additional bar, redesigned by Marsh Grochowski Architects), while the upper courtyard forms an extension to the bar, with new translucent canopies placed over the bar seating area. The impact of the square has been to engage the theatre more closely with the increasingly lively city centre, and to establish connections between the performing and visual arts.

CASE STUDY

D.H. Lawrence Pavilion University of Nottingham

Marsh Grochowski Architects 1998–2001

The site of the D.H. Lawrence Pavilion, close to the south entrance of the University of Nottingham's Highfields campus, was occupied for seventy years by a tea pavilion (which was later turned into a gymnasium) designed by P. Morley Horder, opened in 1928 and burned down in 1998. Horder's Trent Building and the Portland Building by T.C. Howitt form a backdrop, set on the hillside above the lake – monumental, if coldly formal, exercises in the classical tradition. The pavilion occupies an exposed site, visible from all directions. The challenge was to create an object in the landscape with a dignity of its own, but which made some reference to its classical context. In the 1920s Jesse Boot imagined the public using the lake for boating and taking tea in Horder's pavilion; the parkland was vested in an independent trust and became a popular 'lung' of the city, a role that diminished in the post-war era.

Three-quarters of a century on, a different sort of interface between academia and the city was envisaged. The university had a considerable archive of material relating to the life and works of D.H. Lawrence, for which it wanted to create a proper home, with space to display items to the public. An invited design competition was held, with a number of nationally known practices submitting proposals, and approaches were made to the Heritage Lottery Fund for funding. This was not forthcoming, but the university resolved nonetheless to develop the scheme in significantly amended form with Julian Marsh, winner of the competition, as architect. As realized, the pavilion contains performance and exhibition spaces as well as a café. Financial support, in the event, came from the European Regional Development Fund and a group of private donors led by Sir Harry Djanogly. The building was completed in May 2001, at a total cost of £2.35 million.

The broadly triangular plan and the external form of the building arose mainly from the mix of spaces and uses it contains and, secondly, from its relationship to the landscape and the pedestrian routes across it. There are three principal elements in the building: the 250-seat theatre, the exhibition space with its displays about Lawrence, and the foyer and café (together with a kiosk for ice-creams and cups of tea) which address the route from the University Arts Centre (a development of the early 1990s by Graham Brown Partnership located on the main entrance road to the east). The great 'upturned boat' of the theatre roof, clad in copper, dominates the composition. The building is set back from the lake; Horder's pavilion sat close to the water. (A pair of lakeside 'prospect seats' from the Horder building, spared by the fire, were retained, and serve to frame the new composition. They flank an external amphitheatre.) The main entrance front, to the south-east, is treated as a colonnade, constructed of white limestone, in a stripped classical manner that recalls the work of the Swedish architect

The Pavilion incorporates a new 200-seat theatre (left). Drawing on a variety of historic sources for inspiration, the building has a playful aesthetic appropriate to its lakeside setting. The copper-clad keel-like roof dominates the composition (right).

Wall's

The project reflects a close study of the landscape of the university campus, the inter-relationship of its buildings and the public routes across the parkland. Two small buildings from the lakeside pavilion destroyed by fire in 1998 were retained as part of the scheme (opposite top).

Erik Gunnar Asplund, a rather more imaginative classicist than Horder or Howitt. By contrast, the theatre, adaptable to a variety of performance scenarios, is clad in black granite, while the façade facing the main university buildings is faced in buff brick and has an unassumingly domestic character.

Marsh's plan is conceived to underpin the idea of flexibility and the interplay between the interconnecting spaces and the activities housed in the building. The café-bar, for example, which looks out to the park by day, acts as the theatre bar when there are evening performances. The informal nature of the spaces is inviting, even to those for whom 'the arts' may sound daunting. Association with local hero D.H. Lawrence also helps to sell the building to a wide audience. This is an intriguing building that wears its references and inspirations lightly, and flies the flag for an imaginative architecture of context in a setting where literal historicism sometimes seems an oppressive presence. It has played a significant part in attracting more visitors to the park, and stimulating interest in its conservation and enhancement as a resource for the public as well as the academic community.

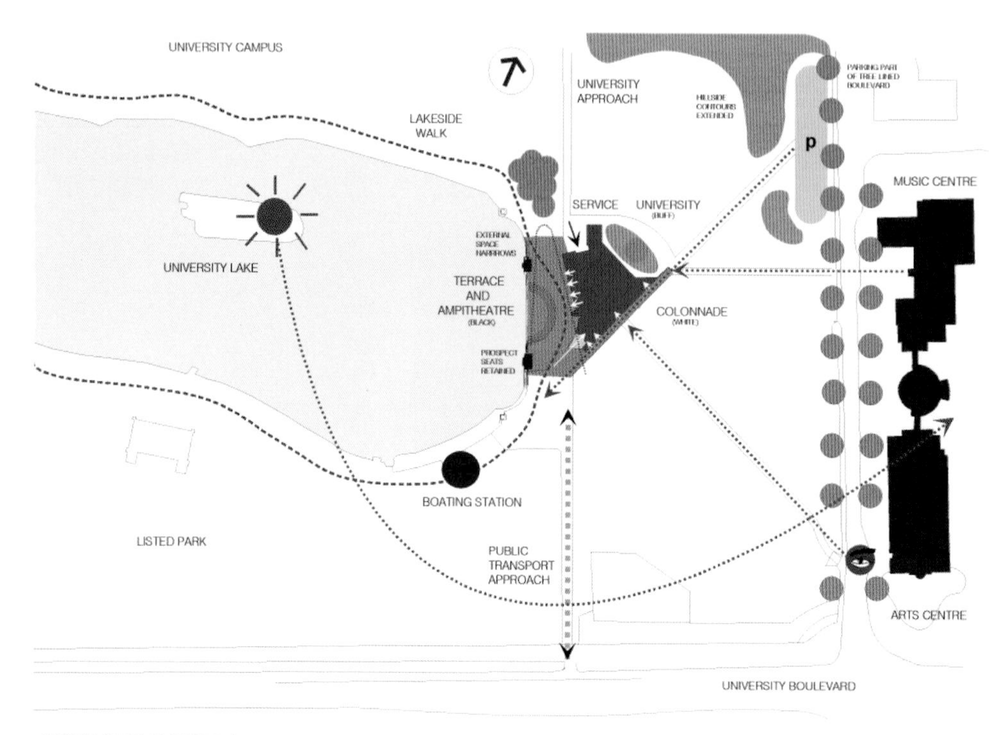

APPROACH TO EMBEDDING
THE BUILDING IN THE SITE

CASE STUDY

Visitor Centre Attenborough Nature Reserve

Groundworks Architects 2004–05

This superb visitor centre has a dramatic relationship with the water and provides an inspiring focal point, greatly increasing public interest in the nature reserve.

Gravel extraction at Attenborough, in the borough of Broxtowe, began in the 1920s. The large expanses of water that have been created as a result form a natural haven for wildlife, and the Attenborough Nature Reserve opened in 1966 under the aegis of the Nottinghamshire Wildlife Trust. It is now a popular visitor amenity, quite apart from its primary agenda of conservation. The visitor centre was the outcome of a 2002 feasibility study that addressed the needs of the nearly 100,000 people visiting the site annually. There was judged to be scope for a considerable increase in visitor numbers, with the proposed visitor building providing information for visitors, educational facilities for school groups, a café, shop and WCs, the development potentially generating a significant profit for the Trust and allowing for improved access and better management of visitors.

'Eco-friendly' was one term that featured in the brief for the building, and Groundworks Architects responded strongly to the prescription in their competition-winning scheme. The bulk of the funding for the centre came from the East Midlands Development Agency (EMDA) and a fund set up by the site owners, with a £250,000 subvention from the Heritage Lottery Fund in respect of the educational aspects of the project and smaller contributions from English Nature and Broxtowe Council. Home store Ikea provided the fit-out of the education room. The building opened in March 2005. By the summer of that year, the centre's visitor numbers were running at double their previous total – around 5000 people each week.

The 'green' agenda of the building is never far below the surface, though it has not been pursued at the expense of aesthetics: this is

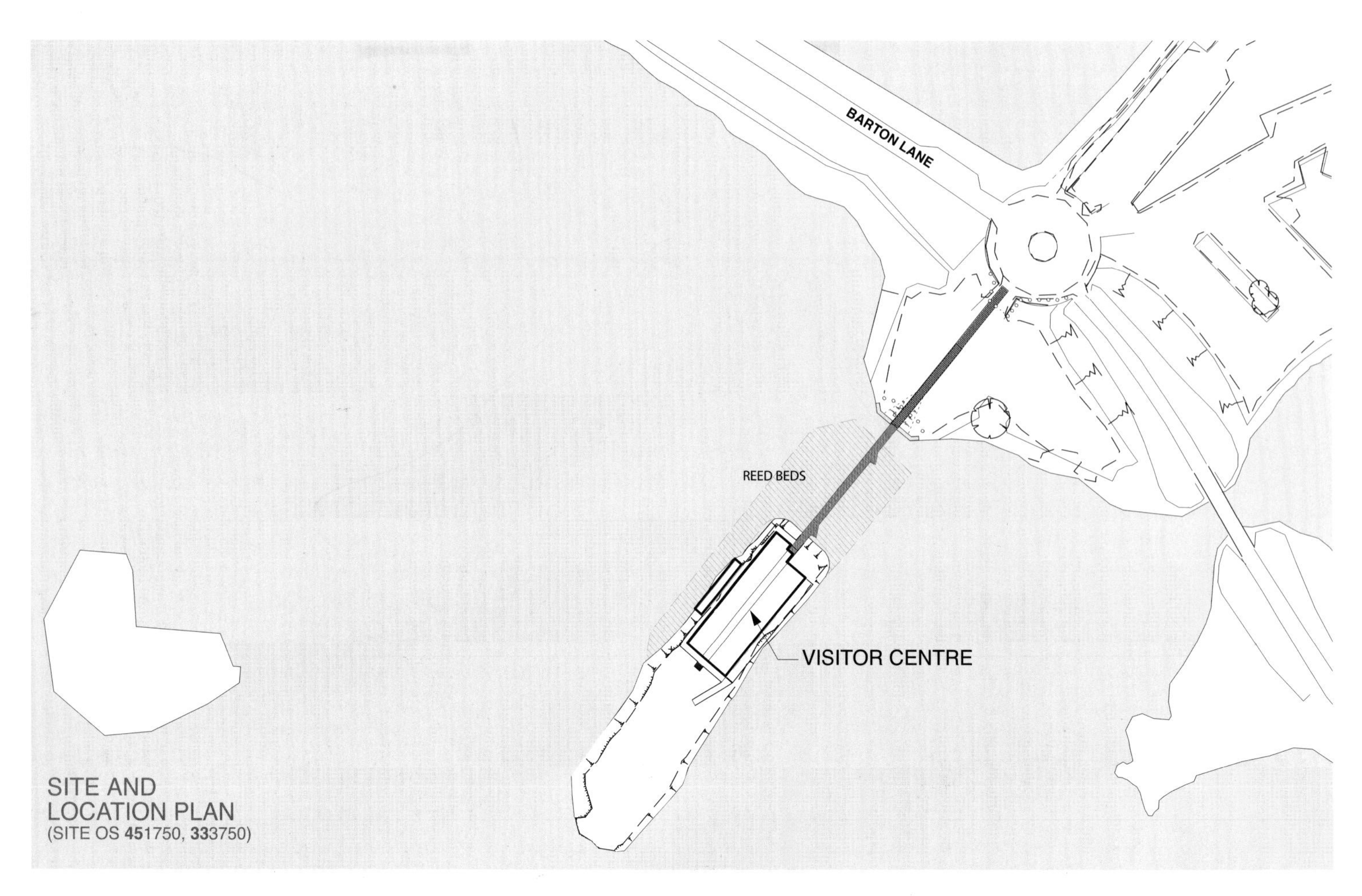

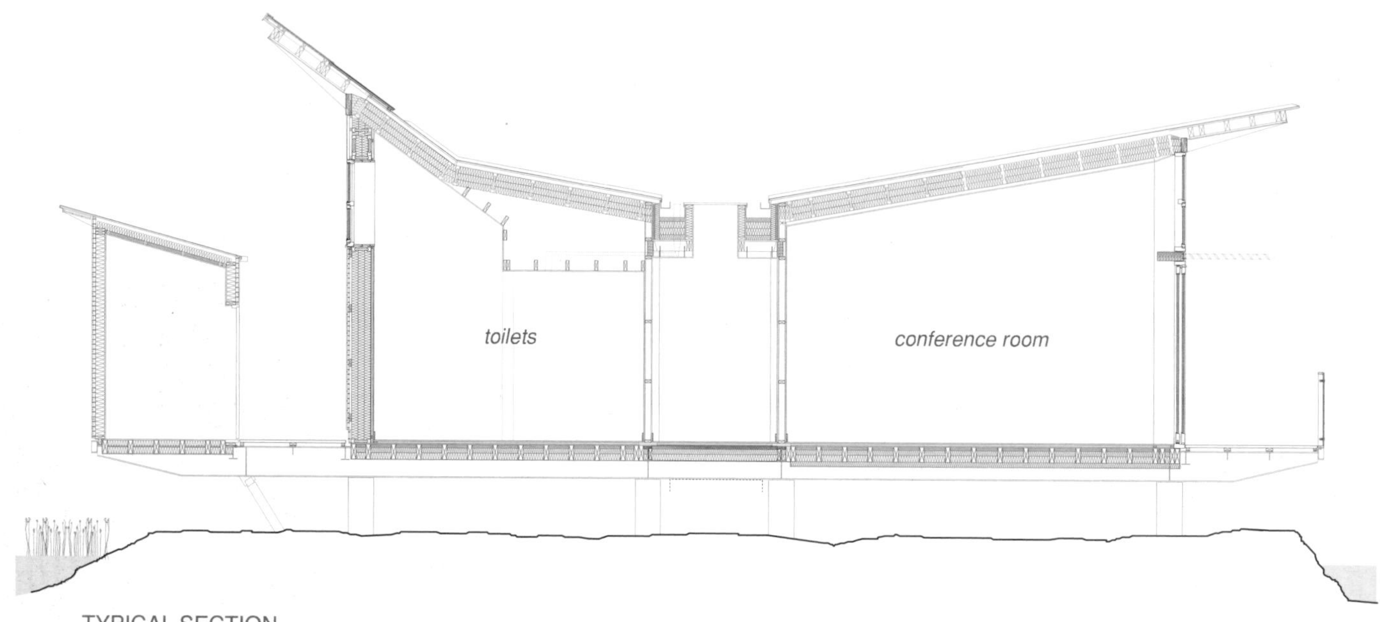

TYPICAL SECTION

a welcoming, well-crafted structure that is a pleasure to visit and work in. It is a lightweight pavilion, sitting in the water at the end of Barton Lane and accessed via a drawbridge that ensures security on this isolated site. Inside are a reception area and shop, café (focusing on locally grown products), meeting room, education room, office, store and WCs. The centre is constructed on a steel frame infilled with well-insulated timber panels and roofed in stainless steel. The imperative to construct the building within six months – to ensure minimum disturbance to breeding birds – meant that extensive use was made of prefabrication off-site. Leeds Environmental Design Associates was involved as environmental consultant for the project, and an environmentally friendly services strategy included the use of photovoltaic panels to generate power, a heat-pump using lake water, heavy insulation and the optimum use of natural light – a display in the reception area carries continuous reports on the energy consumption and generation of the building. EMDA, in particular, demanded a building that would act as an exemplar of good environmental practice and, within the constraints of its modest scale, the Attenborough Centre meets the brief.

The building is set within the lake formed by the flooding of a former gravel pit and approached across a pedestrian bridge. It is a simple, well-crafted structure of timber on a steel frame, heavily insulated and appropriately embodying high standards of environmentally friendly design.

The New Art Exchange Gregory Boulevard

Hawkins Brown 2005–07

As the UK's first regional inner-city arts centre devoted solely to the promotion of the arts from ethnic and minority groups, the New Art Exchange will be a cultural landmark. The site is in Hyson Green, a relatively poor area of the city and the subject of an ongoing regeneration campaign, with a late Victorian church (now a community centre) and public library for its immediate neighbours, and an ugly 1960s block of flats rising behind.

Partly funded by Arts Council England, the building will contain workshops, galleries, rehearsal rooms, meeting rooms, education facilities, and a café and shop. An innovative aspect of the scheme will be the involvement of resident artists in developing the detailed designs for the building in association with Hawkins Brown. Its strong and simple form making the building a local landmark, the New Art Exchange is designed as a welcoming, open, environmentally friendly community resource. In 2005 the scheme, described as "community architecture without the earnestness", won project architects Seth Rutt and Harbinder Singh Birdi a slot in the RIBA's *A.J. Corus 40 under 40* exhibition.

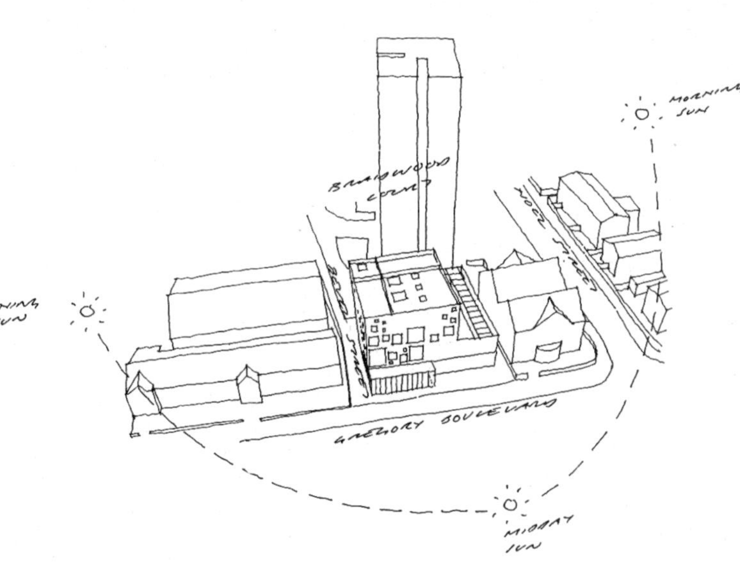

The Art Exchange is designed to contain a number of different spaces for varied activities (above). The transparency of the new building will encourage participation and create a new focus for the community (opposite top). Site sketch (opposite bottom).

MUJI
MUJI
OUTDOOR

City of Leisure

City of Leisure

Half a century ago, Nottingham was an industrial city, bolstered by the core manufacturing industries – bicycles, pharmaceuticals and tobacco – that had seen it through the difficult inter-war years, and with older industries, notably textiles and coal mining, still important props to the regional economy. Today Nottingham is essentially a post-industrial city, in which new, office-based service industries are increasingly significant sources of employment, along with central and local government, the National Health Service and two booming universities.

It would be idle to pretend that problems of unemployment, poverty and deprivation do not exist in the Nottingham region, but the city's generally buoyant economy has fuelled a continuing tide of investment in 'leisure industries', serving an affluent, often youthful population with increasingly sophisticated tastes. A few decades ago, there were few restaurants in the city centre. Pubs were glum places catering largely for the older generation; hotels were for businessmen. Few came to Nottingham for pleasure, though there was always an influx for Test Matches at Trent Bridge and two football clubs drew sizeable crowds from the surrounding area. A hundred years or more of slum clearance had removed virtually all housing from the city centre and its immediate confines. Post-war clearances underlined the divide between the city centre and the suburbs where most of the city's population lived, with the 'semi' as most people's ideal.

In the first decade of the twenty-first century, Nottingham is in the midst of a transformation that has made the city centre (which is steadily expanding) a destination for patrons of opera, film, theatre and concerts, clubbers, food-lovers and those simply wanting a convivial evening in a pub or bar. Thousands now live in or very close to the centre of the city, walking to work or to the cinema, bar or restaurant. City living has become fashionable, and not only for the young – some older couples are selling large suburban houses for a new life conveniently close to the city centre's facilities. Students, for too long driven into poor-quality accommodation in houses more suitable for family use, are colonizing new developments like the Student Exchange next to Sneinton Market.

Trent Bridge, a historic Test cricket ground, has been rejuvenated by the construction of the new Fox Road stand (above), which was opened in 2002.

Nottingham city centre (opposite) is one of Britain's principal retail destinations, with a range of small and large shops set within a substantially unchanged framework of historic streets.

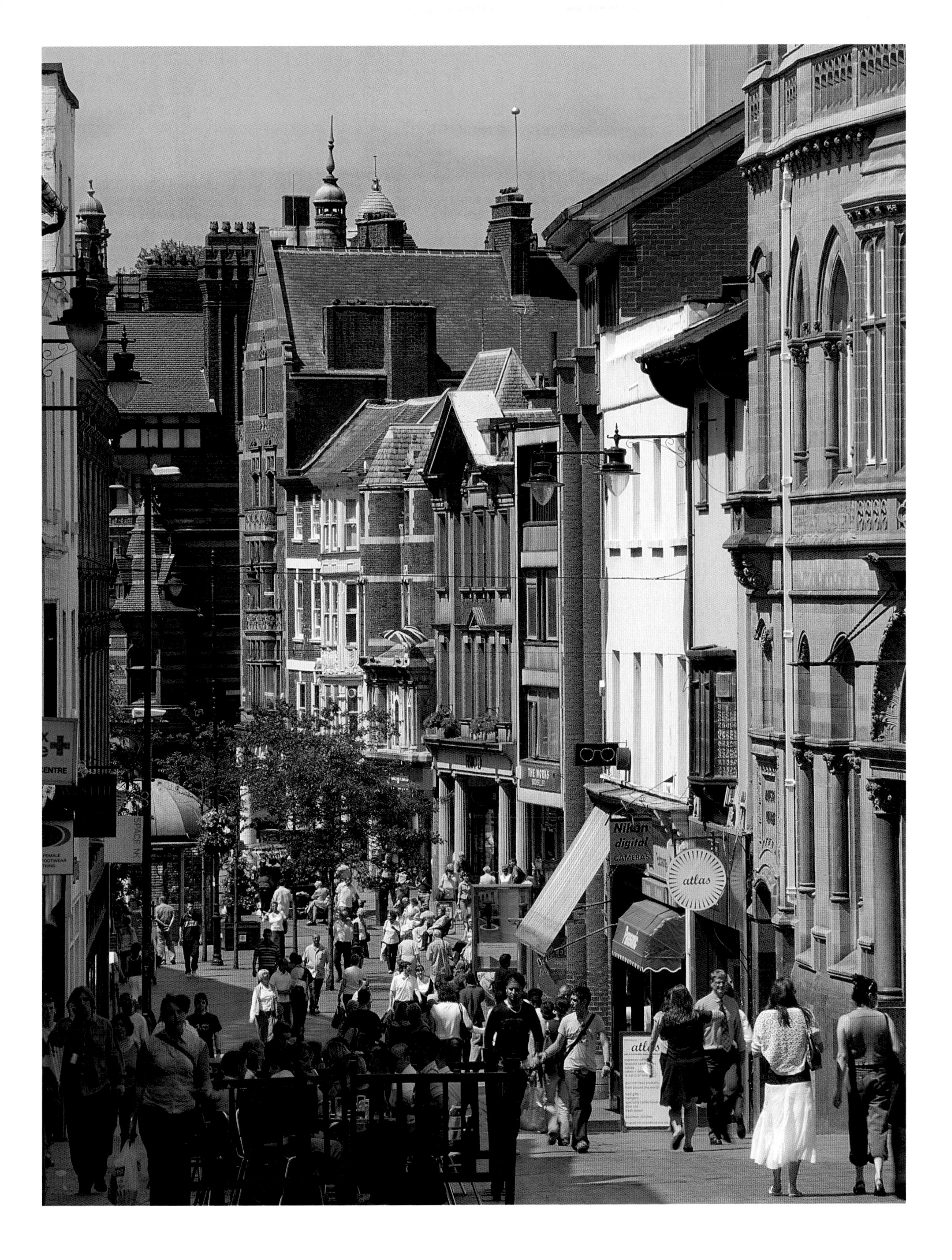
THE WORKS
Nikon
digital
CAMERAS
atlas

One Degree West (opposite), a dramatically proportioned house by Marsh Grochowski, is a rare modern intervention into the Park's Victorian townscape. The Graham Brown House on Park Terrace brings a touch of West-Coast glamour to the Castle escarpment (top left and right). Lace Market Properties' proposed Litmus apartment block (above) on Huntingdon Street is now on site.

Individual new houses have set a lead with innovative ideas for city living – Graham Brown (formerly of William Saunders & Partners) set a striking example with his 1980s house on Park Terrace, one of three houses he designed along the edge of the escarpment which form a bold statement of modernity in the context of the historic suburb. Writing in Country Life magazine in 1993, Neil Jackson compared the house to the classic steel-framed houses of America's West Coast: "Here, where the sandstone cliffs are as steep and unbuildable as any in the Hollywood Hills, [Brown] has elevated his house on slender steel legs and projected lightweight balconies beyond the gardens below." In 1995 architect Julian Marsh completed a new house for his own occupation in the Alexandra Park Conservation Area, a building that responds to its suburban context without needless deference. (Another Marsh project in the same vein is the One Degree West house on Western Terrace in the Park, completed in 2004 for local developer Bill Hammond.) Having since sold his own house, Marsh has acquired a site in the Meadows, close to the city centre, where he is building a 300 sq m (3230 sq ft) live/work, low-energy house on the site of a single-storey 1930s factory in Felton Street. Marsh sees the project as about "encouragement by demonstration", a positive contribution to the regeneration of the area, with its architecture an exercise in "responsive contextualism". The low-energy strategy of the project is serious: a ground-source heat-pump, solar collectors, heavy insulation and recycling of water and waste are part of a didactic agenda. The same progressive thinking infuses Marsh's designs for a new house (in fact, a radical transformation of a derelict industrial building) in the Lace Market, commissioned by Nottingham South MP Alan Simpson. At a total of around £300,000, the 'eco-house' costs no more than a decent suburban semi, but is designed to cope with rising energy costs and make its own contribution to countering the effects of global warming.

Not everyone can live in the city centre but its shops, bars and restaurants are a regional magnet, generating a great deal of high-quality interior design alongside the more standard formats of the chain operations. In fact, the city's wealth of old and interesting buildings has proved attractive to big fashion retailers such as Zara, FCUK, Jigsaw and Reiss, who operate from stylishly refurbished premises in historic streets rather than units in large shopping centres. Nottingham's newest, most stylish hotels include

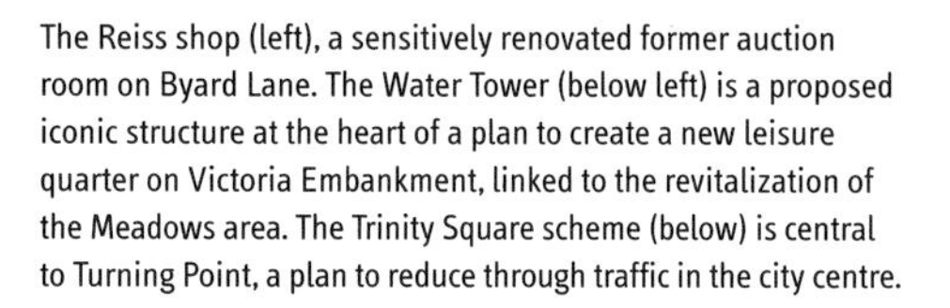

The Reiss shop (left), a sensitively renovated former auction room on Byard Lane. The Water Tower (below left) is a proposed iconic structure at the heart of a plan to create a new leisure quarter on Victoria Embankment, linked to the revitalization of the Meadows area. The Trinity Square scheme (below) is central to Turning Point, a plan to reduce through traffic in the city centre.

the Lace Market Hotel, housed in converted buildings, as well as Marsh Grochowski's Hart's Hotel (see pp.158–61) that forms part of the transformation of Standard Hill.

There are elements of continuity in Nottingham's leisure scene: football, of course, and cricket. (Maber Associates' Fox Road stand at Trent Bridge, completed in 2002, has seating for 2321 and epitomizes the new generation of comfortable and stylish sports venues.) The new Ice Arena, opened in 2000, replaced the old 1930s arena where Olympic champions Torvill and Dean trained. More than half-funded by money from the National Lottery, the £40 million, 7000-seat centre was designed by the City Council's own architects with Arup engineers, following a competitive tender process. It is a big, bold structure in the high-tech tradition, with a flexible main arena that can seat nearly 10,000 for big pop concerts with the rink covered over, filling a major gap in the city's line-up of venues. A second, 'community' rink opened in 2001.

This is the kind of facility that could very easily have been exiled to the city fringe. Locating the development close to the Lace Market on the eastern edge of the city centre, adjacent to the key Eastside regeneration zone, with a clear assumption that its audiences would depend largely on public transport, was a progressive move. The building could not, by its nature, be 'contextual' – some may find it an abrasive intruder – but its regenerative credentials are impeccable.

An artist's impression of Benoy's Waterside development (opposite top), part of a major plan for the city's river Trent frontage. The Ice Arena (opposite bottom) between the Lace Market and the Eastside.

Santa fe
sausage
world
CINEMAS
Saltwater
flaming dragon
oriental cuisine
Virgin
ACTIVE

CASE STUDY

The Cornerhouse Forman Street

Benoy 1998–2001

Occupying a sensitive site close to the Theatre Royal and Guildhall, the Cornerhouse development (opposite) contains a dazzling mix of leisure facilities and provides a new meeting-place (above). The impact the building makes on the city was prefigured in this striking drawing by cartoonist Burke (above right).

The Cornerhouse, a highly successful development containing a sixteen-screen cinema complex, nightclubs, cafés, bars and restaurants, occupies a key site directly opposite the Theatre Royal and Royal Concert Hall, and complements the more conventional version of 'culture' purveyed by those institutions with a mix of strongly youth-orientated leisure facilities.

The site was formerly occupied by the former premises of the Nottingham Evening Post and a series of small shops along Trinity Row; the relocation of the Post opened the way for the redevelopment that effectively defined this sector of the city centre, north of Upper Parliament Street and close to the Nottingham Trent University campus, as Nottingham's leisure quarter.

The Cornerhouse was nothing if not ambitious in scale (18,580 sq m/200,000 sq ft at a cost of over £40 million), and inevitably had a significant impact on its surroundings. In fact, Forman Street, where the 'front door' of the development is located, contains a series of small-scale buildings of no special distinction. To the east is the 1880s Guildhall, a formal, stone-faced composition in French Renaissance style with its principal elevation to Burton Street. On South Sherwood Street, to the west, the Cornerhouse faces the angular glazed frontage of RHWL's concert hall. The architecture of the scheme represents a response to this variegated context, though the urge to create a crowd-pulling landmark is also to the fore. The south-west corner of the site, where the building addresses the junction of South Sherwood Street and Upper Parliament Street, was the obvious place for exuberant display, and the frontage here is formed of lightweight materials, with plenty of glazing – escalators inside whizz people up to the cinemas at the top of the building.

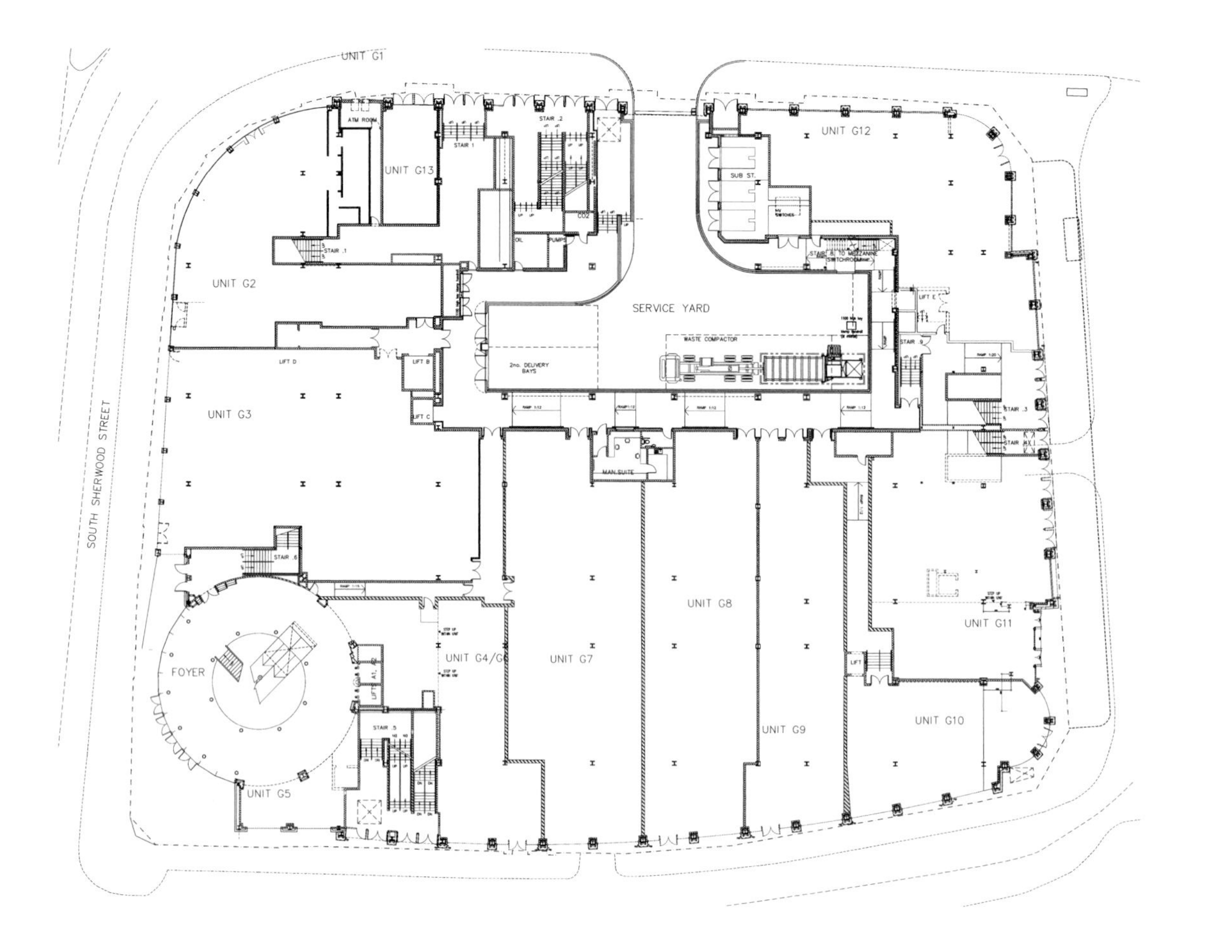
UNIT G1
UNIT G13
UNIT G12
UNIT G2
SERVICE YARD
WASTE COMPACTOR
UNIT G3
SOUTH SHERWOOD STREET
FOYER
UNIT G4/G6
UNIT G7
UNIT G8
UNIT G9
UNIT G10
UNIT G11
UNIT G5

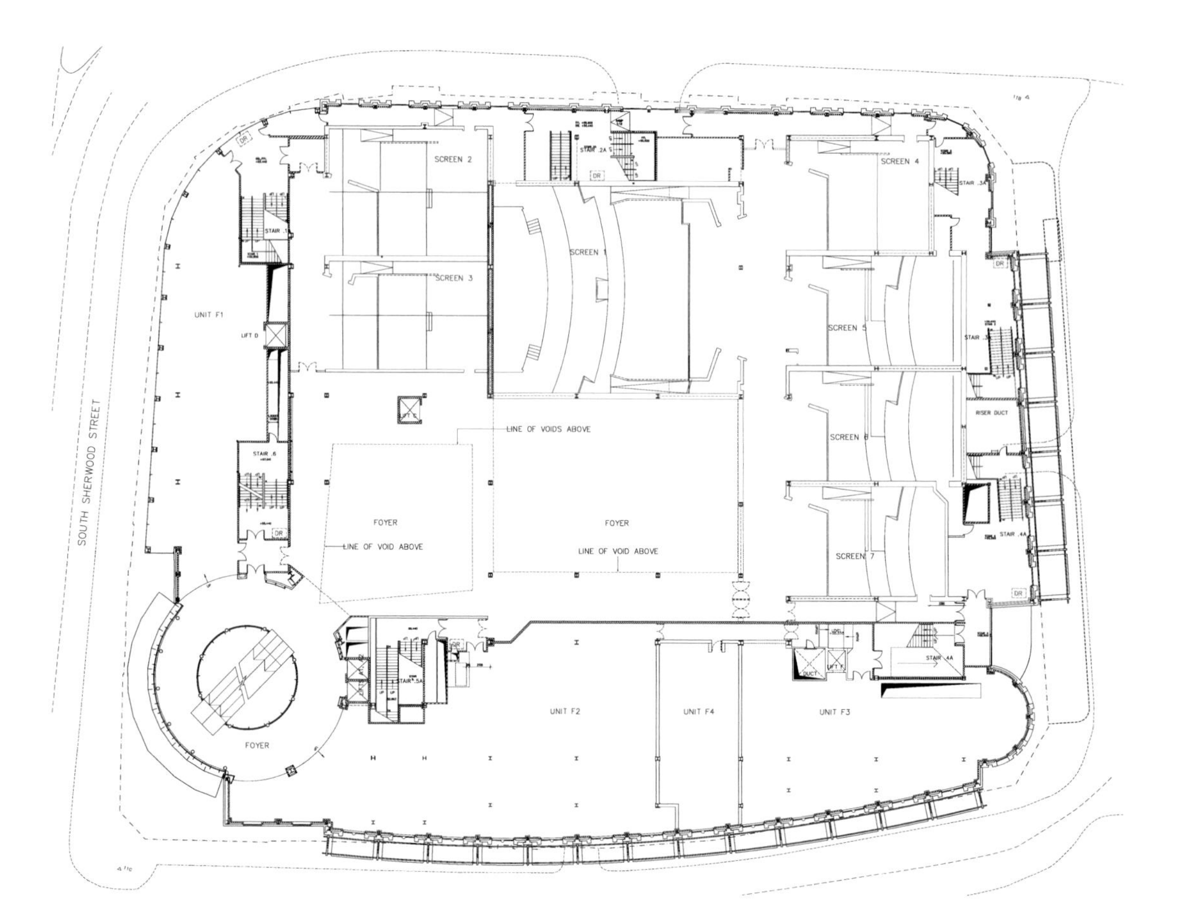
SCREEN 2
SCREEN 1
SCREEN 3
SCREEN 4
SCREEN 5
SCREEN 6
SCREEN 7
UNIT F1
SOUTH SHERWOOD STREET
LINE OF VOIDS ABOVE
FOYER
LINE OF VOID ABOVE
FOYER
LINE OF VOID ABOVE
RISER DUCT
UNIT F2
UNIT F4
UNIT F3
FOYER

Elsewhere the façades are formed on a base of stone, chunkily detailed, becoming more transparent as they rise up the building. One clever move was to set back the cinema 'boxes' from the perimeter, so that the façades have windows lighting circulation routes and are not unrelieved masses of masonry. On the Forman Street elevation, the stepped form of the building allowed for the creation of south-facing terraces for restaurants on the upper levels, a good place to survey the city.

The building includes external terraces (above) which look out over the city, while its transparent façades (left) allow daylight and views to penetrate.

Nobody pretends that this is great architecture. Like the super-cinemas of the 1930s, it is about fun and escapism. The interior is glitzy, with a significant 'wow factor'. Fit-outs of the units within the development vary in quality, but it can safely be predicted that most will be recast many times in the life of the building. In terms of the city centre's renaissance, however, the Cornerhouse has made a significant contribution and works well as a decent piece of urban fabric.

HART'S
HOTEL

CASE STUDY

Hart's Hotel Standard Hill

Marsh Grochowski Architects 2001–03

Not so many years ago, the typical provincial city hotel was generally part of a large national (or international) chain, and delivered a predictable product to a largely corporate clientele. In those days, hotel restaurants, good or bad, were one of the few options for dining out in the provinces. In the last couple of decades, however, Britain's major cities have been transformed, and Nottingham is no exception. Hart's Hotel reflects the renaissance of the city centre as a place not only to do business but equally to live, dine and generally enjoy life.

The first obvious fact about Hart's is that it is the outcome of an individual's vision, and not a corporate product. Tim Hart had run a successful restaurant for some years in part of a converted hospital building on the edge of the Park. The welcome decision that the General Hospital would close completely, with the site redeveloped as a mix of housing and offices in new and converted buildings, provided the spur to Hart's next venture, to open a 'townhouse' hotel on land adjacent to the restaurant.

The site was both rich in potential and problematic. It enjoyed wonderful views over the Park, and beyond to the Trent valley. But there were constraints too: a run-down Georgian house, long used as a doctors' mess, presented a hurdle to redevelopment, and the case for its demolition had to be made. There was also the prospect of serious archaeological remains being uncovered – this was the site of the long-lost postern gate of the castle – and there were the ubiquitous caves beneath the ground. The impact of the hotel project on the Park Conservation Area also had to be carefully considered, with the listed Park Terrace immediately to the west of the sloping site, with the Park Steps alongside, and the fanciful Tower House and gatehouse to the north.

Marsh Grochowski Architects' scheme provided for a 'pin-wheel' plan that responds both to the historic context and to the contours of the site. A four-storey wing facing south-west over the Park, containing guest rooms and the reception, takes its cue, in terms of scale, from Park Terrace, and to the north forms a composition that takes in Tower House and the gatehouse. A second four-storey block extends further south-west and contains more guest rooms with fine views across the valley – windows are recessed to reduce the overlooking of the nearby Park Terrace gardens. The third wing of the 'wheel' is three storeys high and reaches out towards Hart's Restaurant in an adjacent building. The main entrance point to the thirty-four-bed hotel is located at the

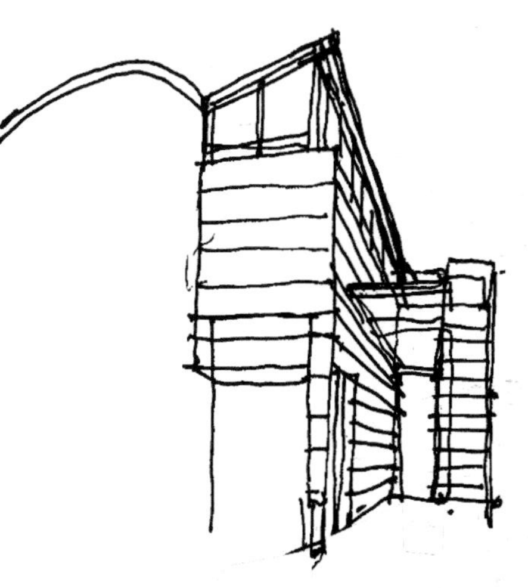

Hart's Hotel is a modern boutique hotel located in a sensitive but dramatic location on an escarpment at the edge of the Park. Its new buildings are sympathetic to the nearby Georgian houses.

The plan of the buildings responds to views out from the elevated site. The detailing of the buildings is simple and elegant with interiors in a restrained, modern manner (opposite bottom).

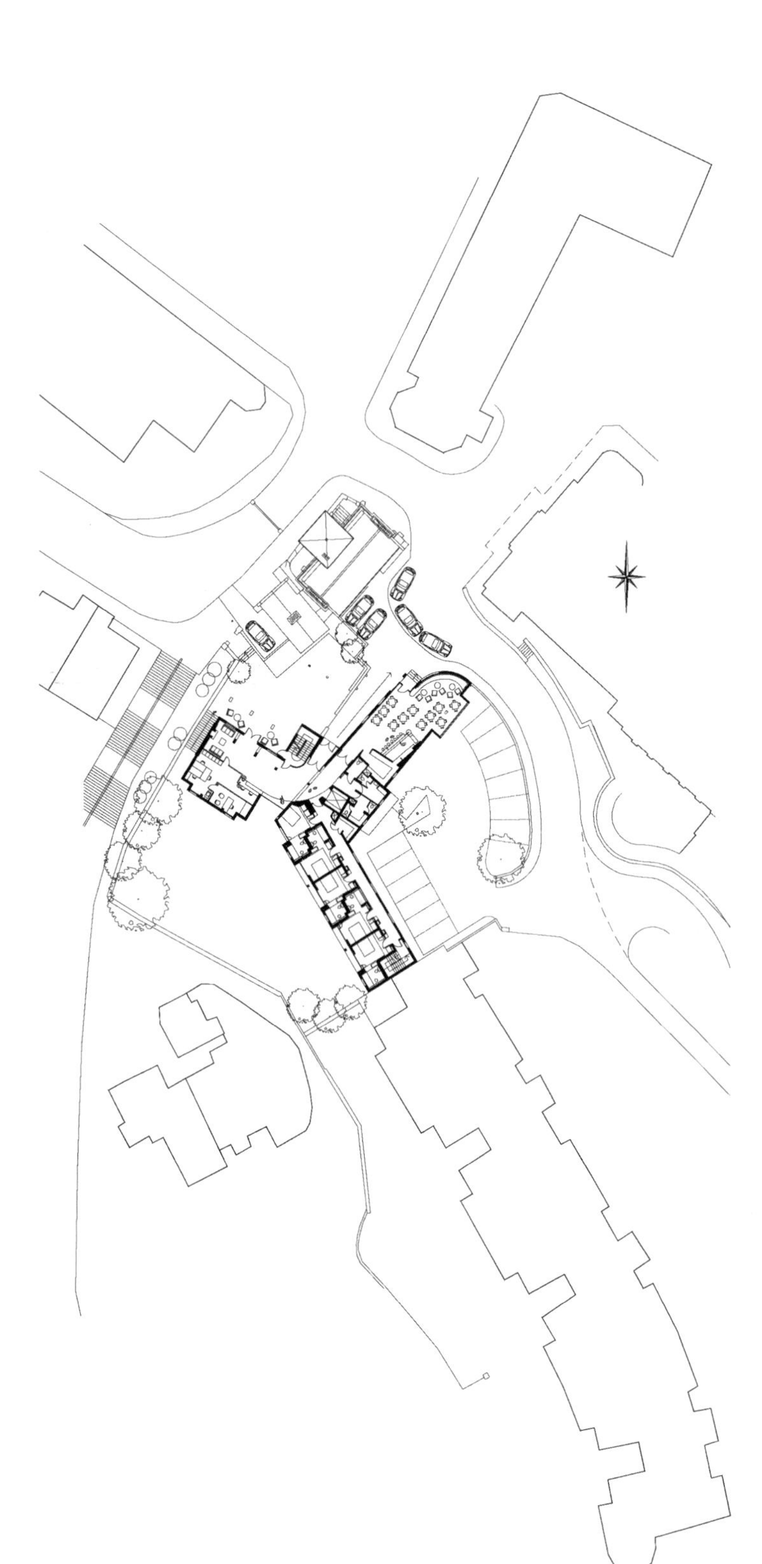

junction of the three wings and is an impressive space with fine views over the Park. Interior decor supervised by Tim Hart's wife, Stefa, is entirely modern in manner, with a number of artworks by Stefa Hart's father, the painter Vladimir Daskaloff, on display.

Internally and externally, Hart's Hotel is sophisticated but never intimidating, an excellent example of the new-generation designer hotel and an important addition to Nottingham's range of visitor facilities. As architecture it reflects the skills of Marsh Grochowski Architects in creating a distinctive modern contextual approach to design that works particularly well in this sensitive location, responding both to the surrounding architecture and to the intense drama of the escarpment site.

PARK
HART'S
HOTEL

CASE STUDY

Willoughby House Low Pavement

Franklin Ellis Architects 2005

The restoration of Willoughby House as a flagship store for the Paul Smith fashion house involved a stylish, high-quality and carefully executed fit-out of the period rooms, including specially designed display cabinets, by Barnard & Wilson.

Willoughby House is one of Nottingham's finest Georgian buildings, clear evidence of the rise of fashionable society in the town during the eighteenth century. It was completed in 1738 (by an unknown architect) for Rothwell Willoughby, third son of Sir Thomas Willoughby, Lord Middleton of Wollaton. By 1764 it had passed from the Willoughby family into the possession of one of Nottingham's first bankers. From 1835 on the house was occupied not as a family home but as office chambers. There were, inevitably, many changes over the next century and a half: the ground floor had been much remodelled, and a new staircase and lift were inserted in the 1950s. On the top floor, the original windows had been replaced with incongruous new glazing.

Nonetheless, a remarkable number of historic features survived, including doorcases, fireplaces, shutters and cornices. On Low Pavement, the fine railings and gates had survived the attentions of Second World War salvage campaigns, though the layout of the forecourt had been much altered.

Nottingham was the birthplace (in 1946) of fashion designer Paul Smith and the site of his first small shop in 1974. Paul Smith Limited is now a leading fashion retailer worldwide. The company had resolved to develop a new flagship store in Nottingham, and was looking for a distinctive historic property suitable for conversion. Its acquisition of the Grade II* Willoughby House was a bold move, given that there would inevitably be considerable restrictions on the permitted degree of change to the interiors, and that all works would require the approval of English Heritage as well as the City Council. The aim was, however, to retain and enhance the domestic character of the house, using the period interiors as a unique showcase for Paul Smith products and minimizing the impact of the new use on the listed fabric. A key feature of the brief was the requirement that display fittings should not be attached to the walls or panelling, but should be freestanding and moveable.

A comprehensive renewal of building services was, however, necessary. Retail use, involving a concentration of lighting, required the use of air conditioning, in addition to ventilation, on the ground and first floors, neatly accommodated using existing ducts with chiller units replacing radiators in window reveals. Voids in the floors proved capable of accommodating all new services. Some of the timber floors had to be upgraded to deal with increased loadings. Another issue that had to be addressed was that of fire safety: smoke lobbies

All historic features were retained and restored, and incongruous later additions and alterations removed. The building, long a hidden treasure of the city, is now being made fully accessible to the public. It includes a superb garden at the back, which can be seen from the shop's windows (opposite).

were formed, using glazed screen/door infills on the ground floor, with existing doors at first and second floors upgraded using seals, intumescent card and paint (the alterations could be reversed should the use of the building change at some future date). All historic features were carefully conserved and repaired where necessary. All existing windows were retained and overhauled, save for the twentieth-century replacements on the third floor, which were removed in favour of accurate reinstatements of period glazing. A new lift, reusing the shaft constructed in the 1950s, provides disabled access – not possible via the main entrance on account of the raised forecourt and flight of steps.

Willoughby House was one of Nottingham's hidden treasures, inaccessible to the public, its fine interiors long cluttered with desks and filing cabinets and dowdily decorated. It is now open to all and is a delight to visit, though the goods on display are as much an attraction to the design-minded visitor as the architecture. Doubtless the project makes business sense, but it reads equally as a generous act of homage on the part of Paul Smith to the city of his birth. As he said when opening the shop in February 2005, the opportunity to achieve something so distinctive in his home town was "absolutely brilliant".

FUTURE PROJECTS

Broad Marsh Centre Reconstruction

Westfield Design Group and partner architects 2007–11

Those old enough to remember the opening of the contentious Broad Marsh Centre in 1975 and to regret its destructive impact on the historic centre will gain a certain satisfaction from its impending demolition, after a life of little more than thirty years. (Many recall Drury Hill, a memorable piece of townscape, removed by the construction of the Centre.) In one sense, of course, redevelopment might seem a wasteful option, yet it offers real gains for the city while being rooted in sound commercial logic. The Broad Marsh – Pevsner found it "unprepossessing" – will certainly not be missed in its present form.

Its featureless architecture apart, the worst aspect of the Centre was its ruthless intrusion into the urban form of the city; the architects for its redevelopment rightly describe it as "a particularly brutal piece of urban planning". Up to the later Victorian period, the area to the south of the centre, around the canal, had been one of squalid slum housing. The opening in 1900 of the Great Central's Victoria Station north of the old centre and the subsequent rebuilding (1904) of Midland Station to the south provided a stimulus for the development of a new north-south commercial axis that remains fundamental to the character of Nottingham today. The Broad Marsh Centre imposed a massive barrier across this axis, cutting off Midland Station and the canal (a backland in the 1970s, now a hive of activity) from the centre. Built, like the Bull Ring in Birmingham, as a megastructure around part of the inner ring-road, it was essentially an internalized development, with no effort made to provide pedestrian links to the castle or to the Lace Market and the neglected eastern fringe of the city centre beyond.

Conveniently, the Broad Marsh Centre is increasingly perceived as a commercial failure, certainly lagging well behind the Victoria Centre as a draw for shoppers. (The 1972 Victoria Centre may not be great architecture but it slots neatly into the hole left by the demolition of Victoria Station.) The multi-level diagram of the Broad Marsh – a consequence of the 12 m (40 ft) fall across the site – results in too many dead ends, and vertical connections are poorly handled. There are too many small shop units that have proved hard to let. All in all, the Centre has ceased to be an asset for the city.

In common with other recent redevelopments of 1960s shopping malls – Birmingham's Bull Ring, for example – the new Broad Marsh Centre is designed not as a megastructure but as a series of city blocks connected by streets, squares and covered arcades. The new Centre, to be designed by Westfield Design Group, Angus Pond Architects, Marsh Grochowski Architects and The Design Solution, will occupy a considerably extended area, requiring the demolition of some surviving Victorian buildings (of modest interest) around the northern end of Carrington Street and Greyfriar Gate. The latter street, along with Collin Street, will be incorporated into the redevelopment, removing part of the intrusive 1960s road network. The masterplan includes an area bounded by Maid Marian Way, Popham Street, Middle Pavement and Canal Street, and provides for around 120,000 sq m (1,291,700 sq ft) of retail, catering and leisure uses, along with a new bus station.

The emphasis is on achieving the permeability that the present Centre lacks, with Lister Gate extended through the site as a grand galleria to Canal Street and hence to Carrington Street, Midland Station and the rapidly developing south side of the city. Central to the complex will be a really generous public square, looking to the castle and lined with cafés and restaurants. The present entrance to the Centre from Bridlesmith Gate and Middle Pavement, the retail core of the city, is distinctly downbeat and will be radically remodelled to create a welcoming threshold. From here a progression of three-level glazed arcades, a new take on a familiar building type, will form the backbone of the development. These arcades will easily accommodate the natural fall in the site, while avoiding the awkward level changes found in the existing Centre, and will connect conveniently to adjacent streets. The creation of new routes through the Centre is a key objective – this will be an extension of the city centre, not a self-contained retail fortress. The developer's decision to commission a variety of architects to design elements of the new complex is commendable, a further indication that the monotonous uniformity of the old Broad Marsh is not to be repeated. This project is a landmark in tackling head-on the problems resulting from 1960s planning, and reintegrating a major element of the city's retail provision into its historic fabric.

The Broad Marsh Centre, opened in 1975, is now regarded as an unfortunate blot on the city centre, and is failing commercially. Plans for the redevelopment of the centre provide for much-increased permeability with a naturally lit central galleria, and shops and restaurants on three levels.

Old Market Square Reconstruction

Gustafson Porter
2005–06

The Old Market Square is the heart of Nottingham, a place of assembly and rendezvous and equally one of passage, straddling several principal axes across the city centre, and linking key destinations such as the castle and the Theatre Royal. Start walking at any point in the city centre and you almost inevitably end up here. Medieval in origin, it housed an open market until the 1920s. With the construction of T.C. Howitt's Council House, replacing the Georgian Exchange, the old market was judged unseemly and banished from the city centre, ending up in the bowels of the Victoria Centre. Howitt's revamped square was a formal composition, focused on a Processional Way leading to the portico of the Council House. Over the last seventy-five years, the layout has been successively compromised. The removal of traffic from Long Row left Howitt's solid Portland stone enclosing walls incongruously isolated in the middle of new areas of paving. The advent of the tram in 2004, routed around the east and south side of the square, has further compromised the 1920s layout. Recently, the relevance of Howitt's complex series of level changes, ramps and steps has been questioned, and in 2004 a competition was launched by the City Council for a scheme to make the square more accessible, usable and enjoyable, while preserving its civic dignity.

Gustafson Porter's scheme, which went on site in autumn 2005, could be seen on one level as a return to the square as it was pre-Howitt – a clear, level, flexible open space that can be used for fairs, markets and performances. The practice was selected from a distinguished shortlist, including both architectural and landscape firms including Gillespies, Hopkins Architects, Stig L. Andersson, Conran and Partners, and Patel Taylor. The range of proposals was broad and it was, perhaps, the straightforwardness of Gustafson Porter's scheme that won the day, proposing a place that is characterized by constant movement (and far easier to traverse than Howitt's complex space), and by areas for rest and events, all within the context of a hard landscape designed for heavy wear. Access for the disabled, an issue that was not on the agenda in the 1920s, has been fully addressed, with gradual level changes to a maximum of a one in twenty gradient, allowing easy wheelchair access. For Neil Porter of Gustafson Porter, the square is a naturally 'organic' space: he feels that Howitt imposed an arbitrary formality on it. His aim, in contrast, was to maintain "a light touch".

The scheme reflects a careful study of the historical background of the square. Gustafson Porter noted in John Speed's 1610 map of Nottingham the presence of a line, possibly the remains of a town wall, slicing across the space. This has been reinterpreted as a drainage grille that, as a dynamic line of movement, ends on an axis with the Council House entrance. The square's northern side receives most of the sunlight and has been designed as an area of stepped plant and seating terraces. Long Row is assimilated into the new space, with steps down to the seating terraces, but retains its distinct identity, reinforced by tree planting, café terraces and the installation of a series of relocated, listed lanterns designed by Howitt. The centre of the square is deliberately kept clear of interventions as a simple paved plane. The south-eastern sector contains the boldest and most prominent new feature, a series of four water terraces stepping down from a reflecting pool, which feeds a dramatic waterfall, to a level where there is just a thin film of water. The terraces can be drained and used, where necessary, as seating for events in the square. To facilitate the use of the square for events, masts incorporating lighting and capable of supporting temporary sound equipment are placed along South Parade.

The choice of materials for the scheme reflects the diversity seen in Nottingham's historic buildings, though granite is used extensively in the centre area of the square and seating terraces, a welcome change from the concrete slabs of recent paving schemes. Planting will help to create a sense of enclosure and reduce the impact of some of the poor-quality twentieth-century buildings visible from the square.

This project is of defining importance for the city centre, both in practical terms – giving the square a new sense of purpose – and for its symbolic value as a statement of Nottingham's civic pride, restated in the vocabulary of the twenty-first century.

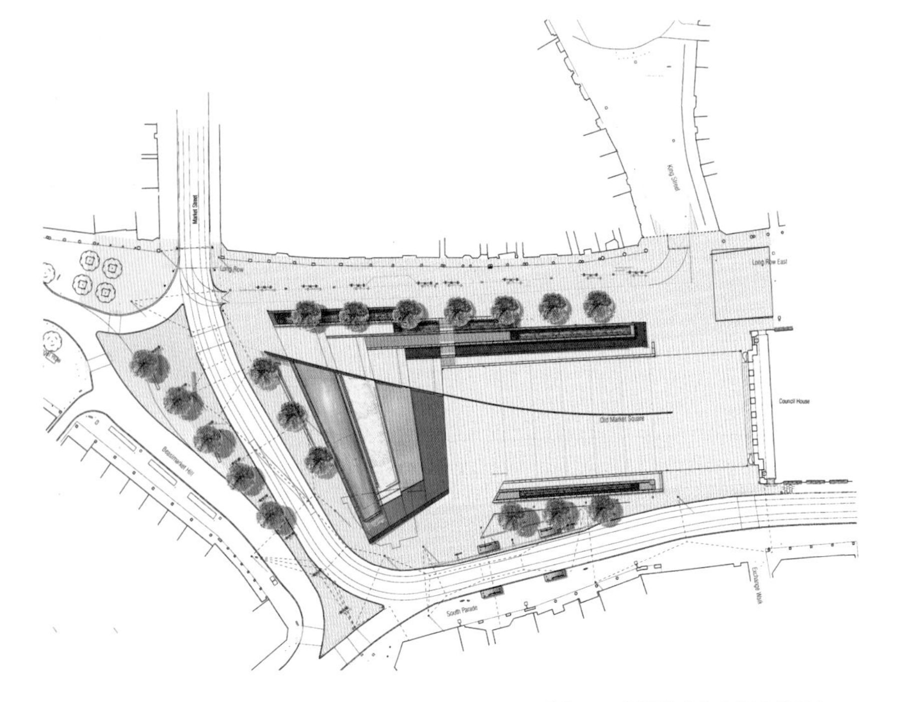

The Market Square reconstruction will replace the now heavily compromised layout by T.C. Howitt. The new space will be flat and uncluttered with a series of water terraces, constituting a more flexible public area.

Afterword

by Councillor Jon Collins
Leader of Nottingham City Council

Dusk views, from the Eastside across the Lace Market to the Castle (above) and towards the Council House (p. 174) show the vibrancy of the developing city. A map from the 2005 city-centre masterplan (right) indicates the vision for the city over the next ten years with the creation of new spaces and development areas.

I hope you have enjoyed reading the story of Nottingham. We are very proud of what has been achieved in the city over the last few decades.

The success and the schemes you have seen in the book are very much the product of the energy and skill of the businesses, universities and public-sector agencies in Nottingham working together. I should like to record my appreciation of what they have done. Many of the projects have transformed the areas in which they are located, and this has been greatly to the benefit of local people.

But our plans for the future, as you can see, are equally exciting, and will further develop Nottingham as a European city.

Nottingham is often described as "two cities": alongside a prosperous and vibrant city centre and a successful economy, there is disadvantage. But there is a powerful drive and commitment to tackle this.

There is a strong, shared vision for Nottingham, and we are determined that the ambitious plans for education, transport, housing and the economy will benefit all sectors of our diverse community. There is an enthusiastic team spirit in the city to achieve that.

I should like to add my appreciation of all those who have helped to put the book together. I hope that it will inspire others to create new projects of the quality that you have seen here.

Environmental improvements
Proposed square
New Transport Interchange
Proposed tall building
Development opportunity
Traffic reduction
City Centre relief route
City Centre bus loop
NET & stops
Improved entrance
Proposed pedestrian connection
Historic building to be refurbished
MANSFIELD ROAD
HUNTINGDON STREET
SHAKESPEARE STREET
DERBY ROAD
UPPER PARLIAMENT STREET
COUNCIL HOUSE
CASTLE
CASTLE BOULEVARD
LONDON ROAD

Bibliography

Architects' Journal, special issue on Nottingham, vol. 205 (5), 6 February 1997

M. Barley and R. Cullen, *Nottingham Now*, Nottingham 1975

J.V. Beckett, *A Centenary History of Nottingham*, Manchester 1997

— with K. Brand, *Nottingham: An Illustrated History*, Manchester 1997

K. Brand, *Thomas Chambers Hine, Architect of Victorian Nottingham*, 3rd edn, Nottingham 2003

— *Watson Fothergill, Architect*, 3rd edn, Nottingham 1997

As Built: Caruso St John Architects, Madrid 2005

K. Coates and R. Silburn, *Poverty: The Forgotten Englishmen*, London 1970

D. Cottam et al., *Sir Owen Williams, 1890–1969*, London 1980

C. Davies et al., *Hopkins 2*, London 2001

A.P. Fawcett, 'A Tale of Two Cities: Sheffield and Nottingham and the Provincial City in Inter-war Britain', *Planning Perspectives*, 15 (1), 2000, pp. 25–54

— with N. Jackson, *Campus Critique: The Architecture of the University of Nottingham*, Nottingham 1998

E. Harwood, *England: A Guide to Post-war Listed Buildings*, London 2003. Includes Boots D90, Cripps Hall, Newton Building NTU and Nottingham Playhouse.

—'"Prestige Pancakes": The influence of American planning in British industry since the war', *Twentieth-Century Architecture* (1), 1994, pp. 78–93 on Boots D90

A. Jones et al., *Nottingham's Heritage*, Nottingham 1985

N. Pevsner, *The Buildings of England: Nottinghamshire*, 2nd edn, Harmondsworth 1979

E. Scoffham, *A Vision of the City: The Architecture of T.C. Howitt*, Nottingham 1992

R.S. Tresidder, *Nottingham Pubs*, Nottingham 1980

Picture Credits

Benoy 156 (both); Benson + Forsyth LLP 52, 53; John Birdsall Social Issues Lib. 20r; Paul Bloomer/ Arup 81t; Boots Company Archive 83 (both), 87t, 88l; Ken Brand 33b; Richard Bryant/ARCAID 81b, 86 (both), 89; Burke, courtesy of the Cornerhouse 155r; Burrell Foley Fischer LLP 131; Caruso St John 54, 55; Peter Cook/VIEW 93tl; Corporate Affairs, Nottingham Trent University 123t; CPMG 51b, 80br; John Critchley/Building Images 37; DEGW 87b; Mark Enstone 132t; Chris Etches Architectural Perspective, courtesy of Franklin Ellis 47; Farey, The Howitt Partnership 28bl, 30t; Faulkner Browns 108b, 110b; Foster and Partners 118–19b; Francis Frith Collection 22, 26; Franklin Ellis 68; Groundworks 140, 142b; Gustafson Porter Ltd 168, 169; Hawkins Brown 144b; /AMPlify Design 144t, 145; Henson & Co./Nottingham City Council 28t; /Picture the Past 42l; Hopkins 64, 98, 99, 113b, 114b, 115m, b, 123b; Howitt Partnership (Nottingham Local Studies Library) 122; David Hoxley 38–39; Letts Wheeler 70 (both); Edgar Lloyd 19, 35bl; John Lock 34; Make 120 (both), 121; Marsh Grochowski 47b, 132b, 134 (both), 138b, 139b, 159b, 160b; Bally Meeda and Rakesh Kumar, Urban Graphics Ltd 171; courtesy of MGM CLIP+STILL 18l; Nottingham City Council 17bl, 18r; /R. Allen, Picture the Past 16r; /BDP 74; /Leisure and Community Services, Local Studies Library 14, 15l, 20l, 48t, 78; Nottingham Evening Post 11; ORMS 93b; Christine Ottewill 130; Sheppard Robson 94, 97t; Edwin Smith (RIBA Archive) 33t; W. Spencer, Picture the Past 42r; F.W. Stevenson, courtesy of Mrs May Sentance 17r, 58r, 128; Surrey Flying Services, Picture the Past 58l; Westfield Shoppingtowns Ltd 166, 167.

Acknowledgements

Author's acknowledgements

I am grateful to Adrian Jones of Nottingham City Council, who has been a constant source of advice and encouragement. Jim Taylor has coordinated the process of research, information-gathering and collating, arranging some memorable visits to buildings and expertly keeping the project on track and on schedule. Vanessa Corns provided invaluable assistance with research and documentation. The historical introduction could not have been written without the very generous assistance of Ken Brand of Nottingham Civic Society, whose publications have so expanded appreciation of the city's architectural heritage. Martine Hamilton Knight, responsible for the great majority of the photographs in the book, and Julian Marsh have been unstinting in their support for the project. I should also like to thank the many architectural practices, owners and occupants of buildings for their help. Finally, my thanks to Julian Honer, Rosanna Fairhead, Helen Miles, Paul Shinn and Sadie Butler at Merrell Publishers.

Photographer's acknowledgements

Thanks to Douglas Whitworth, Ken Brand, Dorothy Ritchie at Nottingham Local Studies Library, Robert Elwall at RIBA, The Boots Company Archive and Picture The Past's East Midlands Photographic Archive, without whose assistance tracing historical images would have been very difficult indeed. A personal thank you to Nottingham City Council, for asking me to be involved in this project. Having spent fifteen years photographing the city's buildings, it is rewarding to see them together in one book for the first time. Also, thank you to the architects and designers who asked me to record their work in the first place. And finally, to my family who have stood patiently by my tripod and computer.

Nottingham City Council would like to thank Graham Brown, Sophie Clapp, Robert Cullen, Christopher Draper, Lynn Hanna, Tim Hart, Wilson Hogg, Neil Horsley, Peter Jackson, John Maslen, Phil Nodding, Dorothy Ritchie, Rob Robinson, Tim Sheil, Philip Songhurst, Jennifer Spencer, Hichem Tranche and Matthew Varley.

Scottish Life
ALBERT HALL

Index

Page numbers in **bold** refer to the illustrations